Also by Sam Levenson

EVERYTHING BUT MONEY

IN ONE ERA
AND
OUT THE OTHER

❀❀❀❀❀❀❀

Sam Levenson

SIMON AND SCHUSTER • NEW YORK

SBN 671-21578-7
LIBRARY OF CONGRESS CATALOG CARD NUMBER: 73-5250
DESIGNED BY EVE METZ
MANUFACTURED IN THE UNITED STATES OF AMERICA

1   2   3   4   5   6   7   8   9   10

ACKNOWLEDGMENTS

Much gratitude to Esther, Conrad, Isabella, and Emily for listening or reading at any hour of the day or night. To my brothers and sister and brother-in-law and sisters-in-law, especially to my brother Albert, who did whatever had to be done. To Leon Shimkin of Simon and Schuster, who urged me to do the book. To Peter Schwed, who urged Mr. Shimkin to urge me. To Charlotte Seitlin, fine editor and fine friend; to Peter Matson, agent, adviser, and friend; to Larry and Sophie Howitt of Seven Hills for letting me try out chapters on their guests; to Dr. Sol Jacobson and Dr. Myrtle Jacobson for their invaluable interest and judgment; to Charlotte Greene, teacher, librarian, and friend for her sharp mind and even sharper pencil; to Frank Metz, Dan Green, Joan Wexler, Millie Marmur, Christine Steinmetz; to Sophie Sorkin, Gypsy da Silva and Elise Sachs; to Dorothy Maltzman; to George and Dorothy Lent; to Philip Kanof for typing and talking; to Jan and Dan Ruberman; to Dave Vern; to the Ladies' Home Journal, Woman's Day, *the New York* Daily News, *and* Reader's Digest *for prepublication use of parts of the book.*

TO
MIKE
AND
GEORGIA
WHO
MISSED EACH
OTHER

CONTENTS

I

Sorry, Wrong Era

❀ ❀ ❀

It was on my fifth birthday that Papa put a hand on my shoulder and said, "Remember, my son, if you ever need a helping hand, you'll find one at the end of your arm." So I took my arm by the hand and off we went to seek my fortune. Show business was the last place in the world I expected to find it.

I almost made it as a child star, but it was not yet to be. My debut was in a kindergarten play at Public School 86, Manhattan. It was on the eve of Chanukah that I brought home the glad tidings. "Ma, tomorrow I'm gonna be the last 's' in Merry Christmas."

"Oy," Mama groaned gratefully.

I got one curtain call, but didn't get another until about twenty-five years later.

In the meantime Mama and I dreamed of my becoming a great violinist—a dream we shared every night. We saw me stage center, in Carnegie Hall, delivering a brilliant performance of a simplified Minuet in G to the cheering and swooning of thirty-five hundred Mama Levensons, one in each seat, and hundreds more on borrowed kitchen chairs all around me on the stage.

My brothers (who never even dreamed of being mothers) found me somewhat less inspiring. "Sammy has such a wonderful memory. He makes the same mistakes over and over again."

They compared me with Heifetz. "A Heifetz he ain't!"

The family next door had a dog who sang along with me. "Do us a favor, Sammy. Play something he doesn't know."

They appointed me "company violinist." If there was company that stayed on too long they turned to me: "Sammy, play the violin."

As in all my careers (I think I'm now in my fourth), I was a late bloomer in music. In junior high school I got to be concertmaster of the orchestra and fiddled well enough to earn spending money with my own dance band, Sam's Snazzy Syncopators. We were "Available for All Occasions," but hired only for a few. Good Old Max, our political leader, engaged us for rallies. We always marched on just ahead of him, blaring out "Mother Machree," "Mamma Mia" or "My Yiddisheh Mama," depending on the neighborhood. He paid very little, but he hinted a lot about getting me into West Point.

The day our synagogue acquired a new Torah, it was paraded through the streets not with the biblical zithers, harps, pipes, flutes, horns, castanets and cymbals, but with Sammy on the solo violin. This time I worked for free. You can't charge God. (Professional courtesy.) Besides, only God could ever get me into West Point.

Perhaps it was in payment for previous services rendered gratis, but a short while later an act of God did occur—a professional booking in St. Gregory's Roman Catholic Church. Neither my parents nor I had ever been inside a church. For me to be invited there was implausible, but to get paid ten dollars for being there was incredible.

Ruth Byrne, my history teacher, hired me to play the Bach-Gounod "Ave Maria" at her wedding. It was an overwhelming experience. I cried throughout the performance, partly because of Bach, Gounod, and St. Gregory, but mostly from inhaling incense. By the second chorus I was ready for my last rites. When I finally made it home, Mama asked only whether the church was bigger than Carnegie Hall; Papa asked whether the priest had worn his skullcap, and my brothers asked if I had noticed any small miracles, like maybe I had played in tune.

Thanks to my band I got to spend a whole summer in the country at a small resort hotel. I must have possessed the quality that soothes the breast of savage beasts. This time it was not a dog but the owner's horse that got carried away by my playing. When I practiced he would stick his head through the broken window of my ground-floor room and neigh along with Sam. When I proudly reported this to the boss he said, "It's not you; that's his room in the winter."

By the time I got out of high school the Depression had set in (I never noticed the change), and unemployed symphony men were underbidding me for jobs. I gave up the dream of ever making it to Carnegie Hall "live" and took the next dream, to college and schoolteaching.

I did make it "live" to my first classroom, but almost did not make it "live" out of it. All my Ed-Psych-Ped-Soc courses had prepared me for teaching but not for this group of teenagers, whom the principal described as "a challenge to a young teacher." I found out soon enough what the challenge was. They were going to test me. If I passed their test I would have the right to test them. I had earned my certification; now I had to earn theirs. It wasn't easy.

"How do you spell Levenson, Levenson?"

"My name is not Levenson. It is Mr. Levenson."

"Oh, 'Mr.' Levenson? You mean you're married?"

"Please write large, Levenson. I can't see the board."

I wrote large. He couldn't see. I wrote larger. He still couldn't see. I finally had my name up on the blackboard in billboard-size letters.

"Now can you see?"

He cupped his hand over his ear and said, "Whadja say?"

The latecomers arrived one by one.

"Why are you late?" I asked each one. (Only a beginning teacher does that.)

"I'm not late; the bell is early. What's the big holler, anyhow? This is the earliest I ever came late."

"Why are you late?"

"I heard the school burned down."

"Then why did you bother to come?"

"I couldn't believe it!"

"Why are you late?"

"It was late when I left home."

"Why didn't you start out earlier?"

"It was too late to start out earlier."

I called the roll and found that one boy was missing.

"He went to the Boys' Room," they told me.

"Why didn't he raise his hand?"

"Raise his hand? How's that gonna help?"

I sent a second boy to find the first boy. The second boy didn't come back. In about twenty minutes I had the whole class out looking for the class. I was afraid to stay in the room all by myself, so I went looking for them too. I couldn't find them. When I got back to the room, there they were, all forty of them, in their seats, waiting to greet me *a cappella* with "Where were you? The principal was looking for you."

I was licensed to teach Spanish to youngsters who took it because "you gotta take a foreign language besides English."

"So why Spanish? We ain't goin' to Spain."

"And how about English? We ain't goin' to England either."

As though it were not enough of a challenge just holding their attention, I was assigned to teaching Spanish in a typewriting room. Each student was seated in front of a typewriter, which each student immediately began to dismantle to take home to remantle.

To keep the typewriters from disappearing piecemeal I invented Spanish Baseball. I moved my desk to the left-hand corner of the room and called it Home Plate. The room was now a baseball diamond. I pitched out a word, a verb, a phrase, and if a youngster "hit it" he went to first base. They hit, they ran, they yelled.

They came to class in sweat shirts and sneakers. I was ahead of my time. The experiment was both an academic and a vocational success. Half the class learned Spanish; the other half learned typewriter repairing.

I taught them their numbers in Spanish by playing Bingo. Each got his turn at calling:

"Treinta y cinco . . ."

"Cincuenta y dos . . ."

"Cuarenta y cinco . . ."

"Yo tengo Bingo."

The losers then broke into the standard four-letter cuss words in English. They wanted me to teach them the Spanish equivalents, but my license didn't permit that kind of curriculum enrichment.

I called in Harry Starfield, a superb teacher and a fair guitarist. I played the fiddle. He taught them to sing about doves ("La Paloma") and I about cockroaches ("La Cucaracha"). Between birds and bugs they picked up the sounds of a foreign language.

If a kid cut school to go to the movies, I would have him stand in front of the class the next day and give a report on

15

what the picture was about, list the cast, and repeat the jokes of the stage-show comedian. Fred Kolmar was the first to break down. He pleaded with me: "I can't do it. I ain't enjoyin' the picture no more. I gotta sit there memorizing." So I excused him from further hooky.

I came to cherish my challengers. I played with them, cajoled them, caressed them, accepted them when they were less than I thought they should be, celebrated with them when they were more than even they thought they could be. The "discipline" was certainly not all it could be, but there was enough of delight in each other to make up for it. They stopped calling me Levenson, or even Mr. Levenson. I had earned their professional certification and their personal respect. They now called me "Teach."

I used to gather all the school humor I could for the faculty luncheons, at which I would "play back" the funny incidents of our academic life. My colleagues appointed me School Jester.

I rewrote and redistributed the principal's circulars to the faculty.

When you receive this notice you are to disregard previous notices 126-A, 126-B, and 316-C. In case you did not get them, send for them immediately and destroy them.

The Fire Law says that if you find a boy student in flames and have no blanket in which to roll him, you are to tear off his burning clothes. If the boy is a girl and you are a man, you must not touch her. You must ask her to take them off herself.

I made up a "typical" teacher's program based on the realities of teaching in a double-session school that started classes at 7:45 A.M.

First Period:	Watch the sun come up.
Second Period:	The class comes into view.
Third Period:	The steam comes up.
Fourth Period:	Wake the children.
Fifth Period:	There will be no fifth period. Instead there will be a special assembly program on homemaking for boys not going to college.
Sixth Period:	Read the following summer-school instructions to the class:

A. Any student may take any subject except:

    1. Those he has passed.

    2. Those he has failed.

B. If any student should ask a question just say, "I'm glad to see you're thinking," and send him on an errand.

I met all the challenges so well that the principal moved me into the Guidance Department. I was given an office the size of a phone booth, no phone, and eight hundred and seventy children to guide. Under that setup it would have been difficult even to misguide eight hundred and seventy children.

My first guidance challenge occurred on the first day of my new assignment. A young girl told me that her friend was "in trouble." I knew and she knew that she didn't mean her friend had lost her report card. It seemed that while her friend had never learned to add, she had somehow learned to multiply.

I was too scared to face this challenge alone, so I talked to the head of the department. She congratulated me on my good judgment and immediately sent for the girl, whom she proceeded to interrogate.

"Is it true?"

"Yes, ma'am," the girl whispered, looking down at the floor, trembling just a little more than I was.

"Is it one of our boys?"

"Yes, ma'am."

"Does he know the condition you're in, my dear?"

"Yes, ma'am."

"Did you talk to him about it?"

"Yes, ma'am."

"And what did he say?"

"He said 'I apologize.' "

It didn't help the girl much, but it proved to me that if you raise a boy to be a gentleman he will always be a gentleman.

As a reward for my helpfulness in this delicate matter I was invited to the wedding. Before the ceremony I called the bride aside and handed her an envelope containing her wedding present. It was my guidance memorandum on the incident. We tore it up together. (Illegal, but merciful.)

As it turned out, the girl really didn't have to get married at all. It also turned out that they really loved each other very much. It also turned out a few years later that they couldn't have a baby of their own, and they came back to me, their counselor, to help them adopt one. I did; and that's how Sam the *consigliere* became Sam the godfather.

It never dawned on me that anyone would give me money to be funny. My school performances had been strictly intramural and strictly for laughs until the faculty of a neighboring school ruined my amateur standing by offering me five dollars—a sum that at the time was equivalent to half my daily earnings and more than half my life's savings. So I became a mercenary. Fun for hire. Have jokes; will travel.

Other groups, civilian rather than Civil Service, began to engage me for luncheons. I went from one charity luncheon to another. These charitable people would gather to eat on behalf of the hungry of the world, so I joined in, being pretty hungry myself. At the luncheons I talked about the familiar in family life, as I had previously stressed the familiar in school life.

"Mr. Levenson's subject for today is: 'Insanity is hereditary; you can get it from your children.' "

The luncheons provided me with humorous material about luncheons.

"Our only speaker today is Sam Levenson. The rest of the program is entertainment."

On one occasion I was asked to follow two minutes of silence "in memory of our vice-president, who passed away this morning. And now for some real laughs from Sam Levenson."

When my fee went up to ten dollars (at my wife's urging) my sponsors got around it by not paying me at all. A man of my importance, they figured, should be honored; so they gave me a bronze plaque as a reward for my noble contribution to their noble cause. When my wife told me that the grocer refused to cash a bronze plaque, I went back to five dollars in negotiable currency.

Meanwhile, back at the school, conditions were well on their way to becoming hopeless. It depressed me to face so many kids who were being deprived of the chance to discover the richness of themselves because of massive schools, minimal budgets, mediocre objectives, and maximal impersonality. I knew I would soon have to choose between staying on and accommodating myself and the children to what was becoming a third-rate imitation of education or taking advantage of my newly acquired forum to improve matters. Perhaps I would end up being a teacher-at-large.

At one end-of-term party a colleague made me an offer: "Sam, we've gotten together an all-teachers' dance band. We've been booked at a summer resort, and we need an MC badly. It's a real challenge. How about it?"

"What will they pay me?"

"Nothing. Only room and board. But we won't have to spend our summer salary check."

"How about my wife?"

"They'll feed her, if you'll clothe her."

"It's a deal."

Afternoons at Arrow Head Lodge I held highbrow lawn sessions on the subject of "Humor and Society," with question-and-answer periods that had to last till dinner time. On show nights I filled the time between the acts in front of the curtain with local-color jokes:

"You know our guest Joe Mackles? Well, he asked his chambermaid, 'Did you find a twenty-dollar bill under my pillow?' And you know what she said? 'Oh, yes. Thank you very much!' "

I would wait for the laugh, run off, open the curtain, work the lights to a blackout on cue, close the curtain, run out, play the violin, tell a joke—"Did you meet our new intellectual guest Bill Davis? At dinner he doesn't eat, he just asks profound questions like '*This* you call chicken?' "—bring on the next act, run off, open the curtain . . .

I repeated the entire procedure the following year with one change—fifty dollars in cash was added over and above the feeding of my wife because she had become pregnant on the premises.

By now I had an act. I tried it out for a few years, then asked the Board of Education for a leave of absence. They would not grant me one except for maternity, so I resigned with the understanding that I could be reinstated within five years, pregnant or not.

My family was stunned.

"You crazy or something? You're gonna quit schoolteaching?"

"Yep, I'm going to seek my fortune in show business."

"Seek your what? You're gonna give up a steady job for a fortune?"

"I enjoy doing comedy."

"You enjoy. But what are we gonna tell the neighbors? Sammy the comedian? For this you went to college? To enjoy? You talk to him!"

It was too late to talk to me.

My son Conrad was about three years old when I broke the news to him.

"I am now a comedian."

"What's that?"

"I tell stories and people laugh."

His lip quivered. "I don't want anybody to laugh at my daddy."

I had to tell him the truth. "They don't always."

My new career was lucrative but hectic. In my heart I longed for "steady" work—for the regularity, order, and long-term friendships I had known at school. But my fellow teachers said, "Sam. Don't come back." A sad commentary on the state of school affairs that so many teachers looked upon me, the teacher dropout, as a hero.

I was still toying with the idea of returning to the academic womb when destiny moved in again, this time in the person of Marlo Lewis, the producer of the Ed Sullivan show, who "caught" me at a banquet.

"How about Sunday, the twenty-fourth, kid?"

"For what?"

"For the 'Toast of the Town,' kid. Be there like four o'clock, kid. Do like six minutes."

"Six minutes?" I asked for fifty-six. He laughed in my face. "The whole show is like only fifty-six-forty, kid."

"I can't do six minutes."

"You'll learn, kid."

The kid learned, not only to do like six minutes but to smile with cables around his feet and booms over his head, in the presence of men with wires hanging out of their ears, stage managers making hand signals in his face, and blinking red-eyed cameras on wheels threatening to run him down. I had reached the point of no return. I had gone from the last "s" in Merry Christmas to the first "S" in Sullivan. Sullivan spelled Success.

The next morning people were talking about "that school-teacher guy from last night's Sullivan show." They hadn't caught the name. "You know, that guy who laughs at his own jokes." (I have always done that, not because I think they are funny but because Papa had told me, "Never depend on strangers.")

I was booked for a repeat with Mr. Sullivan. My mother-in-law told her butcher: "Watch the Ed Sullivan show Sunday night. You'll see my son-in-law."

He didn't believe her. "Your son-in-law is Ed Sullivan?"

Irving Mansfield put me on "This Is Show Business." My name was coming through now. People talked about that schoolteacher guy, "you know who, Sam Livingston, Sam Leverson, Sam Stevenson." I was invited to cocktail parties jammed with celebrities. I was the only one there I had never heard of. I even became the butt of a joke by George S. Kaufman. We were leaving a TV studio when he spotted three little old ladies with shawls on their heads coming toward us down the street. He pointed them out to the director: "Here come Sam Levenson's writers."

After each TV shot I would go back to Pitkin Avenue, Brooklyn, to get the reactions of my old neighborhood friends.

They were more than loyal. "We don't care what anybody says, Sammy. We liked you."

A woman stopped me on the street. "I need a big favor. My sister is finally getting married, Sam."

"Congratulations. What can I do for her or for you?"

"Sunday afternoon is the reception, you know, upstairs at the Little Oriental."

"Yes. I know. You want me to entertain your guests . . ."

"No. I would never impose on you. You see, on their side they have a lot of cousins who are judges and doctors. We ain't got nobody important. All I want is that you should come and sit on our side with us."

I not only went but I posed as their cousin. I did my part, but this marriage didn't last. It seems that their cousins weren't judges and doctors, and the judges and doctors weren't cousins. As the bride's mother told me later: "You're our cousin, Sam, so I can tell you. Such fakers! You can't believe anybody these days."

❀ ❀ ❀

My first nightclub engagement was at the Latin Quarter in New York. I was back on the nine-to-three schedule, except that it was now 9:00 P.M. to 3:00 A.M.

Opening night was SRO—Sam's Relatives Only. Neither my relatives nor I had ever been in a nightclub before. They made it a smash for me, but almost ruined the owner. They didn't drink; they ate rolls. Between rolls and seltzer they polished off the minimum. The busboys had to bring in rolls from the Copacabana and the Martinique. My relatives were the talk of the trade for weeks afterward. "Airlift Rolls" even made the Broadway columns.

From there I went on to the supper clubs of Las Vegas, Miami, Los Angeles, Chicago, and more and more and more.

In Chicago I got to know the club owners and their buddies, the boys in the back room. When I came to work each night they would stand up and greet me with "Good morning, Teach," then go on to sing:

> Good morning to you,
> Good morning to you.
> We're all in our places
> With bright shining faces.
> Good morning to you,
> Good morning to you.

Only when I said "You may be seated" would they sit down.

Like my first class, this group, too, was a "challenge." One night I found a revolver in my tuxedo pocket while I was on stage. They put a sign on my dressing room door: NO HUSTLERS OR SCHOOL TEACHERS ALOUD. They had a six-foot-two Amazon stripteaser "recognize" me as her former teacher, run on stage, and give me a bear hug before a packed house. But if any customer dared to heckle me, his life wasn't worth a plugged nickel. "Get de bum outadere. He's bodderin' de 'teach.'" They each called me "Teach"; I called each "Mister."

Every night they pretended to be unhappy with my performance. "Sorry, Sam. You gotta stay after school." We talked for hours. (The Guidance Department again?) Most of these men were school dropouts who never before had been able to approach a teacher on a one-to-one basis except in hostile confrontation. They sought in me an explanation, perhaps even a reconciliation.

They confessed their past involvement in gang wars, violence in the streets, mob vengeance. To make sure I would understand they took me on pre-dawn visits to the very streets in which the events they described had taken place, to show me the bullet holes in the walls, the jail cells, the escape alleys, the cellar hideouts. They taught this "teach" a couple of things about life he had not learned at school.

When it reached the point where I found myself coming home from work at about the same time I used to leave for work during my teaching days, I decided to give up night school and try again for the old nine-to-three. My eyes slowly became readjusted to the sunlight and I began writing my first book, *Everything But Money*. It did so well that I changed my listing in the Yellow Pages from Comedian to Humorist and raised my fees. I had finally gotten the family off the hook. They could now face the neighbors with "He's a humorist."

At the same time I received a citation that finally got my conscience off the hook, too. I no longer had to feel guilty about deserting the schools. It came in the form of a bronze plaque presented by a national education organization. It read: *To the man who has done more for the teaching profession since leaving it than when he was in it.*

※ ※ ※

Along with Papa's "if you ever need a helping hand" advice, he often threw in, "And remember, if you want your dreams to come true, don't sleep."

I followed the American dream, often at the price of sleep. It left me more time to work on my dreams. I figured that after my dreams came true I could always catch up on my sleep.

My dreams did come true. In fact, it is the truth that has been causing me a good deal of insomnia. Every silver lining has a cloud.

It's this way. I started out in one era and arrived in another. The trip took half a lifetime. By the time I got to my good old dream castle at the end of the rainbow, it had been condemned and replaced by something more up-to-date in prefabricated temporary contemporary. The times had changed.

I met all the challenges, reaped the rewards, and now find

myself with everything a man could ask for, including an outstanding collection of doubts, misgivings, and ambivalences in all sizes.

I had carried on my back into the promised land of milk and money a heavy bundle of attitudes left over from the old days. Call them beliefs, values, conditioned responses, emotional blocks, or what kids today call hangups.

I'm not sure whether I got here too late for the old world or too soon for the new one. I am hung up between two eras. My hair is getting gray, some of it from aging, some of it from the falling plaster of venerable institutions crumbling over my head.

Take, for instance, the institution of money . . .

II

Poor Sammy's Almanac

Having no money to leave me, my parents left instead a rich legacy of attitudes toward money, all based on the premise that while money isn't everything, the way you spend it may determine everything, so spend it wisely, and if you can't do that, be wise and don't spend it at all, because if you spend it, you won't have it for a rainy day, and since you can't tell how many rainy days there are going to be, don't spend even on rainy days, and also put aside something for cloudy days, drizzles, mists, and "who knows what."

Frugality was not just a good habit; it guaranteed a good life. A frugal boy would surely become a prosperous man. The American way was to frugal your way up the ladder of success.

You started by collecting rare coins—like pennies, for instance. "A penny is a lot of money if you haven't got a cent," Mama said. Mama herself was an extravagant saver. She saved more than my father earned.

A penny saved was not just a penny earned. A penny saved saved a person from the humiliation of dependence upon others. "You can't hold your head high with your hand out."

My parents' dread of debt has never left me. Their overwhelming fear was to die owing people money. To come to their Creator with unpaid debts was to come with unclean hands.

One day, when a man from the public library came to our house and told Papa that his son Samuel Levenson owed twenty-eight cents for a lost book, Papa asked what would happen if his son Samuel Levenson couldn't pay. The man said he would be sent to jail. And Samuel Levenson's father said, "Take him away!" Brother Mike ransomed me, in return for which I became his prisoner. He sentenced me to shining his shoes for free for seven years. Whenever I forgot to do the job, he threatened to turn me in to the nearest Public Library.

Mama not only saved money but children.

In school we learned one kind of arithmetic; at home another. $1 + 1 = 2$ was fine with our teacher, but not good enough for Mama. She demanded to know $1 + 1 = 2$ what? Mama's was a method of remedial arithmetic aimed at remedying our poverty by judicious spending. It worked something like this: 1 pair of skates $= 12$ violin lessons. Cancel out the skates and carry over the lessons. She balanced the equations on her scale of priorities and made sure the needle pointed to our future.

> 1 phone call $= 1$ carfare to a museum
> 4 movies $= 1$ shirt
> 1 bicycle $= 10$ pairs of eyeglasses
> 5 ice cream sodas $= 2$ pairs of socks

It was a form of reverse budgeting, planning ahead not only for what not to buy but for buying the instead of, which she could not afford not to own. This kind of juggling, borrowing from our desires to meet our needs, forced minuses to become pluses and liabilities to become assets. She knew the world would never examine her books, but it would examine her children. (She had only one set of these.)

Papa's remedial arithmetic allowed for one cigarette per day, in the bathroom, half in the morning (with you know what) and half in the evening (with or without you know what.) The evening half was left on the windowsill until he got home from work. By the time Papa got to it, it was more like a quarter than a half. We kids practiced on it in the daytime until Mama caught us. She lined us up against the wall for a mass execution and pronounced the last words:

"Look, you wanna smoke, smoke! But I want you to know what's gonna happen. First you'll smoke, then you'll gamble, then you'll drink, then you'll buy a gun, then you'll hold up a grocery store, then you'll kill somebody, then you'll go to Sing Sing, then you'll go to the deathhouse, then you'll go to the electric chair—and then you'll first smoke!"

(To this day I'm afraid to light a cigarette in a chair with arms.)

Today's poor are being lured into participating in the privileges of our opulent society by contributing their last full measure of patriotic prodigality. The pendulum has swung from "Spend what you have left after you save" to "Save what you have left after you spend."

My personal pendulum often swings way back. By contemporary standards I am an eccentric. I still frugalize. I use a penny to pry open a can of shoe polish, knowing that a dime works better. I save R.S.V.P. postage stamps from invitations to which I do not R.S.V.P. In restaurants I read the menu from right to left. In a taxi I watch the meter, not the sights. I shut off running faucets in the park. I automatically put out the light when I leave a room, even if it isn't my light or my room. I have done it at Madison Square Garden, in the men's room at Radio City Music Hall, and in public elevators. (Sometimes there was screaming from the dark I left behind me.) I always close the refrigerator fast, sometimes even before I get what I was after. I also worry about whether the little light inside has gone out, but I won't open the door a second time to check. I still scout around in my car for ten minutes looking for a parking meter with four unused minutes.

My habit of checking gas burners is traceable to the day Mama took her eight kids to visit Aunt Lena. Before we went anywhere Mama always asked us to check the gas burner under the hot-water boiler in the kitchen. This time no one had. When we got back not only was the boiler steaming but Mama started to steam too. Before we could close the door behind us Mama belted out two orders: 1. "Somebody shut off the gas!" 2. "Everybody into the bathtub!"

I must admit that survival through saving sometimes dulled the conscience while it sharpened the claws.

Call it cunning, or call it self-preservation, the truth is that we were sometimes guilty of penny larcenies.

If children through the age of five could ride free on the trolley, what father's child would ever turn six?

"When will I be six, Pa?"

"When you get off the trolley."

It wasn't easy for a kid to remember his various ages: six at home, seven in school, five on the trolley.

Fathers never dared to hit kids on trolleys. "If you hit me, I'll tell the conductor my real age."

There were conspiracies of silence between fathers and kids. "You mustn't lie, but you don't have to tell the truth either. Just keep your mouth shut."

"How old are you, son?" the conductor would ask.

No answer.

"I said, 'How old are you, boy?'"

No answer.

"How old could he be?" said the Papa. "He can't even talk yet."

When there was no longer any hope of passing for a child, we learned to leap onto trolley platforms and to sneak under turnstiles. We also mastered the alchemy of converting copper pennies into nickels. You placed a penny on the tracks and allowed it to be run over by a trolley. This spread the penny to the size of a nickel, which could then be inserted into a turnstile. Some kids sold these penny nickels for two cents. I didn't. That would have been dishonest. I used them myself.

I was with Albert the day he blew his carfare on a frankfurter and made me an accomplice to his crime.

"You," he ordered me, "you're my brother. You're gonna sneak me onto the trolley."

I did. While I distracted the conductor by dropping some pennies, which he helped me pick up, Albert sneaked under the chain and made it to a back seat.

The conductor made a body count and discovered that he was one fare short, a situation that he proceeded to rectify at once, in full view of Albert, who sat there eating his frankfurter while the conductor put a little old lady off the trolley.

Out-and-out stealing of money was out. Every penny in your pocket had to be accounted for. Albert had seen me find one and turned stool pigeon because I had refused to split with him. Mama frisked me and found the penny.

"Where did you get this penny?"

"I found it, Ma."

"Go give it back before Papa comes home."

"Ma, I found it. It's my penny."

Mama began to wring her hands. "That *my* children should be crooks! Go give it back!"—and I got a slap.

Here I was with hot money on my hands and an unacceptable alibi. I went out to the street looking for somebody to give it to. I grabbed the first kid I could find: "Here's a penny, crook. Go home and tell your mother somebody gave it to you, and *you* get killed." He wouldn't take it.

We practiced various types of extortion.

Being sick could be very lucrative. I was never as wealthy as when I was unhealthy. The year I got the whooping cough I made a small fortune. A mother of eight kids could be blackmailed into a payoff if you put up a large enough fuss about taking medicine, especially if you knew how to draw the blood away from your face by pressing your buttocks together, roll your eyes convulsively, and gasp, "I won't take that poison for any money in the world." "Money" was the first clue. If Mama didn't go for the bribe, you continued with "I'd rather die first." "Die" was the second clue. You knew she wouldn't let you die. "Here's a penny. Take the medicine." You could figure out how sick you were by how high your mother would go. I was once so sick they let me hold a quarter in my hand for a half hour. It brought my temperature down immediately.

Relatives who visited our home could be counted on for a present of a penny—a hard-earned penny. Uncle Louie would affectionately twist your cheek between his thumb and forefinger, clockwise, till your right eye moved up to your hairline and the left down to the cleft in your chin (in the manner of a cubist painting), slowly but firmly extracting your molars while checking on your character.

"Are you a good boy?"

You tried to answer, with your tongue now where your nose used to be. "Yesh, Ahma goo bloy."

"You listen to your mother?"

"Allatime lishen m'mudder."

"You good in school?"

"Velly goom niskool."

And we stood there hemorrhaging, swallowing blood and pride, taking it all, never daring to hold out a hand (that would be begging), while Papa would say, "They don't need money."

Maybe *he* didn't need it. *I* would need it—for a doctor.

Uncle Louie came through. Blood is thicker than water.

"Did you say 'thank you' to Uncle Louie?"

"Fank shoe, Uncle Looing."

It was possible to ask Papa for a penny if you had lots of time to listen to his questions:

"You want a what? . . . Who gives me pennies? . . . You're a good asker. Maybe you should work for the United Jewish Appeal? . . . You mean I have to pay you for living with us? . . . You mean you want your inheritance now? While I'm still alive? You can't wait for me to die? Just for that I'll cut you off without a dollar." (Where Papa, who didn't have a penny, was going to find a dollar to cut me off without remained a puzzle to me.)

Asking was not only unproductive but in bad taste.

"Just because you asked you're not gonna get."

"Papa, I'm not asking."

"Good. If you're not asking, I guess you don't need it. Congratulations."

Threatening Papa certainly didn't work.

"Give me a nickel or I'll run away from home!"

"I won't give you a penny, and you can take your brother Albert."

Mama was kinder. "Sure. Find my pocketbook."

The FBI couldn't have found her pocketbook, but this gave us a project for the day: Mission Pocketbook. And if perchance you did find it, there was nothing in it. "Yeh, that's life," Mama would sigh. "All life is like an empty pocketbook." At other times life was like a cup of tea, a pebble in your shoe, a loose door knob, a bell without a tongue, or like an onion. "You peel away layer after layer, and when you come to the end, what do you have? Nothing."

I learned early that if life was going to be like getting a penny for nothing, life was going to be pretty tough.

We had a permissive father. He permitted us to work. Moral support was all Papa could afford to give us. We had to earn what we yearned for.

He was impressed by a newspaper story reporting that the movie canine Rin Tin Tin earned over $200,000 dollars a year. "And we had to have children," Papa lamented in the direction of Mama.

Papa admired anybody who worked like a dog, and if we didn't, he hounded us: "You waiting for opportunity to knock on your door? Maybe she doesn't know where you live. Our name fell out of the letterbox last year yet. Go knock on her door. Wake her up."

"I'd like to go to college," brother Joe said to Papa, and Papa answered him, "Somebody's stopping you?" So he became a doctor. When Jack told Papa he wanted to become a dentist, Papa said, "Good. I could use one."

You could apply, if necessary, to the Levenson Scholarship Foundation, a mutual-assistance fund run by the brothers and sister, which extended noninterest loans for sums ranging from five cents to a hundred dollars for periods ranging from "till tomorrow" to "when I get on my feet." And so it went, with David, Dora, Mike, Bill, Albert, Sammy, not all to college, but all to work. And if you came back without a laurel wreath on your head, you simply had not worked hard enough. Our failures and our successes, Papa insisted, were our own fault. (That relieved Papa and God of a great responsibility.)

Papa had never heard of the Horatio Alger superboy hero, that all-American shoulder-to-the-wheel, nose-to-the-grindstone surmounter of obstacles, indomitable overcomer, scaler of impossible heights, bootstrap puller-upper, so we told him.

"You know what the hero did, Pa?"

"What did he do?"

"He started by shining shoes, and in one year he made a million dollars."

"A million dollars? He must have used very little polish!"

For Papa, Abraham Lincoln was an even greater hero image. The cabin (which reminded Papa of his own childhood), the beard (very biblical), the poverty ("Like me, Lincoln was born without a penny in his pocket"), and above all, Lincoln's respect for hard work.

Often Papa would prod us with, "You know what Lincoln was doing at your age?"

We knew what Lincoln was doing at Papa's age, but we knew better than to bring it up.

One day the ghost of Abraham Lincoln paid a visit to Papa's tailor shop while I was there helping him. My job was not only to press pants but to go through the pockets first to make sure they were empty. "Sammy the pickpocket" my brothers called me. I had already had one disaster when I steam-pressed a white jacket that contained a chocolate bar with nuts.

A customer walked in and handed me a suit. "Just a minute, sir," I said and proceeded to empty out the pockets. To our mutual surprise I found a ten-dollar bill in the jacket. I turned it over to the man with a flourish. (In my head I could hear the heavenly trumpets.)

"Sir, this is yours," I said, remembering how young Abe Lincoln had walked three miles through the woods to return the change a customer had forgotten on the counter. I remembered, too, that young Abe later became President of the United States. Perhaps I would ultimately be rewarded for my honesty. Maybe America was now ready for a Jewish President, Honest Sam. Who could tell?

The customer was quite impressed and offered me a dollar reward. I turned it down dramatically, taking two steps back to make sure my father could get a clear view of the sterling character of his son the President. I loudly announced: "Thank you, kind sir. But it is my duty to return your money. I cannot accept any reward for honesty."

The man left with the money.

Papa was duly impressed. He put his arm around my shoulder and said, "My son, what you have just done makes me proud to be your father—but I'm ashamed to have such an idiot for a son!"

Brother Bill one morning ran out on Horatio, Lincoln, and Papa. He disappeared from Papa's tailor shop and was found in the cellar of our tenement.

"What happened?"

"Not me," he mumbled. "Maybe one of you guys—not me, boy."

"What are you talking about?"

"I was in the store pressin' somebody's sweaty suit when— I don't know how it happened—I feel somebody tappin' me on the shoulder. I turn around and it's Papa and he is lookin' straight at me, and he's saying', 'My son, some day all of this will be yours!' "

As young American hopefuls, we tested the rags-to-riches

formula by embarking on small capitalist enterprises. Since we had the requisite rags, we were already halfway there.

By the time I was eight I had made the classic juvenile deal with a perfume distillery. The magazine ad said in loud print: WIN . . . ABSOLUTELY FREE . . . A TWO-WHEEL BICYCLE . . . SIGN HERE. All I had to do was sell fifty bottles of perfume. I signed here. How could I miss? After all, what kid on my block couldn't use perfume?

The kids wouldn't buy, so I turned to Mama.

"Perfume?" she said. "What is it for?"

"Ma, the ad says it makes women more attractive to their husbands."

Mama looked at her eight kids and smiled a little like the Mona Lisa. "I think I've attracted enough for a while," she said, but she bought a bottle, which she never opened. She gave it to the janitor as a tip for fixing the stuffed toiled bowl. He smelled it, then drank it on the spot.

I found unpublicized virtues in the perfume. It removed ink stains from pants, cleaned eyeglasses, killed cockroaches on contact, and cleared toilet bowls without the aid of a janitor.

Ten months later I still had forty-five unopened bottles. Letters from the Party of the First Part started to arrive:

Dear Sir:
    We hope your sales efforts have proved fruitful . . .

Dear Sir:
    Please remit herewith such funds as you have already accumulated . . .

Dear Sir:
    We shall have to refer this matter to the attention of our attorneys . . .

Finally my pen pal from the company showed up in person to meet the Dear Sir. He asked some civil questions, he got some civil answers, and they started a civil action. Fortunately the court calendars are very slow, and my case hasn't come up yet. There are about twelve hundred kids ahead of me—including forty-three Levensons, twelve of them called Sam.

❀ ❀ ❀

It was a schoolteacher, Miss McGregor Miss McGregor, who launched me into the world of high finance. Anyone who ever had her as a teacher will remember her as Miss McGregor Miss McGregor. In her great desire to make gentlemen of us (including the girls), she would never accept a "Yes" or "No" answer, or even a "Yes, ma'am" or a "No, ma'am." We had to "Face front, eyes straight ahead, hands at your sides" and say "Yes, Miss McGregor," or "No, Miss McGregor." And if you forgot, she would say, "What's my name?" and you said, "Miss McGregor, Miss McGregor."

Tapping the desk with her ruler to get our attention, she announced, "If you will all be quiet, I have some good news for you." We got quiet very quickly. Good news could mean that she was going to be absent for a week, or that "Bring-Your-Mother-Murphy," the school disciplinarian, finally had to bring his own mother to school, or the compulsory education law had been declared unconstitutional. It was none of these.

"Our class is going to embark on a banking campaign in association with the local bank."

"What do we have to do?"

"All you have to do is put money in the bank."

"That's nice," we agreed. "Where do we get it?"

"Well," she suggested, "you can save part of your allowance."

"What's an allowance?"

"An allowance is the money your father gives you."

"Oh." We nodded, and covered our mouths to stifle our

laughter. I knew right away that I could never tell my father that a teacher was talking such nonsense. This was a little like the time she had asked Bernie Gassman, "How many legs does a grasshopper have?" and he said, "Oh, boy, teacher, I should have your worries," and got sent to the principal.

But whenever the teacher said "bank" she could bank on me. From that day on I was not to be found in class.

"Is Levenson absent today?"

"No, Miss McGregor Miss McGregor. He's downstairs in the school bank."

In the morning I would put in two cents and take out one In the afternoon I put in three, took out two. Before long I had three bank books stapled together. I wrote inspirational editorials for the *Bank News:* "Mighty Oaks Out of Little Bankbooks Grow." I was the Benjamin Franklin of the school.

Finally it came—a summons from the bank, not the school bank but the mother bank, THE bank, which was the final repository of the result of our banking campaign. They wanted to meet that supersaver, Samuel Levenson. I could see my picture in the newspapers receiving the Poor Richard Award.

I put on my Sabbath blue serge, walked (naturally) four miles to the bank, at the door of which I was met by three men in Sabbath suits who greeted me with "Levenson?"

"Yes, sirs."

"Father's name Hyman?"

"Yes, sirs."

"Mother's name Rebecca?"

"Yes, sirs."

"Do us a favor, young man. Take your money out of the bank. We've got four accountants working on your books."

I withdrew my eight cents, stormed out of the place, bought a hamburger and a root beer, and was bankrupt. To this day I refuse to deposit any money in that bank.

III

Get a New One

❀ ❀ ❀

When I got to be a teacher I was assigned to the neighborhood in which I had spent much of my early life. I was shocked when I walked into the school Lost and Found Office for the first time and came upon a treasure of eyeglasses, pens, pencils, purses, sweaters, sneakers, skates, belts, ties, teeth braces (some with teeth in them), all unclaimed. The new era had moved into the old neighborhood. "There goes the old neighborhood," I said to myself.

According to my puritan Jewish upbringing, dissipation of earthly goods was decreed and decried as a sin against man and God. I saw (and, in fact, still see) the luminescent finger of God pointing down at me through a break in the clouds and heard (and still hear) the awful indictment reverberating through the heavens: "Hey you, hey kid, hey Sammy. What's that you're throwing away? Everybody, look at him! Wait till I tell your mother! Will you get it from her! Mrs. Levennsonnn!"

When I was given something new, let's say a hat, I took it as one takes a wife—to cherish and protect, in sickness and in health, for poorer or richer, for better or worse, until death do us part.

I shall never forget the terror in my heart the day I lost my hat. I knew that I would have to appear before a family inquest, where I would attempt to plead for my life—hopelessly, since no one in that clan believed that such a loss could be accidental. It could not be anything but premeditated and deliberate, or at least precipitated by contributory negligence.

The trial usually took place at the dinner table before the meal, with an older brother accusing me before Papa as presiding judge, Mama as district attorney, and a jury of my brothers, some of whom had only recently finished sentences of their own and were relishing being prosecutors rather than prosecuted.

Each took a crack at my story.

JUDGE: How do you lose a hat?
ME: I didn't lose it—it just disappeared.
JURY: (*in the style of Gilbert and Sullivan*): It just disappeared!
JUDGE: How does a hat disappear?
ME: I don't know . . .
JURY: He doesn't know!
JUDGE: What do you mean you don't know?
ME: It just wasn't there!
JURY: It wasn't there!
JUDGE: Where was it supposed to be?
ME: Where I left it.
JURY: He left it!
JUDGE: How come you never find a hat?
ME: 'Cause I'm not lucky.
JURY: You can say that again!
ENTIRE CAST: For losing he's very lucky!

41

The final verdict was moral rather than legal, which made appeals impossible.

PAPA: Thank God I have a rich son who can throw things away.

MAMA: Let's say he gave it to the poor.

PAPA: It's a wise boy who knows that in the end we leave everything behind, so he started today with his hat. God, who provides for us all, will provide hats for him to lose.

MAMA: He's got it too good, too good, too good . . .

Papa then dramatically cut a slice from the end of a loaf of bread on the table. His eyes fixed on me rather than on the blade, rocking with religious fervor, he declaimed: "Blessed art Thou, O Lord our God, who bringest forth bread from the earth, even for the wasteful. You may now eat." I couldn't. That blade had slit my throat.

❀ ❀ ❀

On graduating from elementary school or celebrating your Bar Mitzvah (whichever came first) you got a fountain pen, which you wore clipped inside what was flatteringly called the wallet pocket of your jacket. The ownership of a fountain pen was proof positive of your arrival into manhood, as were such secondary characteristics as ink stains on your jacket, shirt, undershirt, and chest.

If the fountain pen symbolized manhood, its loss was the equivalent of losing your manhood. One thing for sure: I no longer slept like a baby. I hardly slept at all. I would wake up screaming, "I lost my fountain pen!" I saw myself coming home from school, opening the door, and hearing my mother say: "I know. You lost your fountain pen."

I became pen-paranoid. I grabbed innocent classmates: "You! You took my fountain pen!" I went completely berserk the day I discovered that I did not lose my fountain pen. It

42

was much worse. I had lost half my fountain pen—the part that writes. What a blow, to be left with nothing but a cap and an ink stain on your wallet pocket. I would have preferred a blood stain.

I am still haunted by the warnings of the mottoes on Mama's kitchen walls: "Waste Not, Want Not." "Willful Waste Makes Woeful Want." I stare in sad wonder at what poor as well as rich families leave on the sidewalks these days for the Sanitation Department to cart away. We are being spoiled faster than our possessions. I see lamps, umbrellas, TV sets, playpens, baby carriages, bicycles, tables, and refrigerators cut down in the prime of life, prematurely junked along with some still good, hardly used values.

We are now in the throes of a throw-away syndrome. "Get a new one"—a new suit, a new car, a new building, a new city, a new country, a new world, a new human race. This one is bent, soiled, cracked, worn, old, dirty, dull. Hurry! Hurry! We must not run out of things to waste. Waste and want . . . Want and waste . . . Wanton wasting . . .

We've been educated to use. We shall now have to be *re*educated to *re*use, *re*store, *re*new, *re*vive, *re*claim, *re*pair, *re*prieve, and respect the earth and the fruit of the earth and the fruits of man's labor.

Mama was a specialist in the resourceful use of resources. She had never heard of ecology. She knew only that if you don't take care of what you have, you won't have it. The prolongation of life was one way of serving God. Resurrection after death was not in our hands; resurrection before death was. Our theology took care of our ecology.

The Levenson Bureau of Reclamation and Redemption was open twenty-four hours a day. Sometimes out of necessity, but just as often out of sheer ingenuity, Mama invented mama-cological uses for things which their inventors had never dreamed of. "If you don't have an education, you have to use your head."

Mama's methods may be reusable. She put everything to work: a little castor oil would make anything go faster—clocks, fans, drills, or kids; a few drops of camphor oil in a steam iron, and you could press a shirt and cure a cough at the same time; the cotton packing from pill bottles was good for an earache; a pair of pants under the mattress at bedtime guaranteed a sharp crease (perhaps four or five of them) by morning; warm laundry water was good for pouring out the window onto those noisy kids; a wedding ring was good for cracking nuts, knocking on steam pipes, prying the cap off a soda bottle, or tapping a kid on the cranium to get his attention; a mixture of flour and water made paste, plaster, or pancakes; matzoh was a temporary filling for cavities; a stale bagel made a first-class teething ring. (To keep bread from getting stale, you had more children.) When Mama caught Albert at the window ready to drop an empty milk bottle onto the head of his best friend Harold, she grabbed his arm in the nick of time: "What's the matter with you? Don't you know that's a deposit bottle?"

A hairpin could be used for getting marbles out of kid's noses, opening door locks, scratching heads, untying knots, cleaning out gas burners, extracting coins from piggy banks, cleaning wax out of candlesticks or ears, turning a screw, opening a wine bottle, removing a splinter, pulling a corset together, plucking a chicken, pitting cherries, and extracting other hairpins from drains. If the hairpins didn't do the trick, a button hook could be used. If the button hook went down the drain, Mama used a hairpin on a string to fish it out. If both went down the drain, you fished them out with a straightened-out wire coat hanger.

The snoring of eight kids, two parents, and innumerable sleep-over relatives took care of the recirculation of the air.

We kids discovered on our own that: used razor blades

could be resharpened by honing them against the inside surface of a glass; a shoe box could be turned into a lunch box, or a home for a turtle, or just a secret vault marked "Private. Keep Out. This Means You." (The local shopkeepers, except for the undertaker, did not mind our asking for empty boxes.)

A wooden box, a plank, and wheels made a racing car. The box came from any store, the shaft from the wrecked building on the next block, and the wheels—well, let's put it this way: we didn't steal them, but if we "came upon" an old baby carriage that looked abandoned (a matter of personal judgment), we liberated the wheels. Let's say we left some kid a sled in place of a carriage. At least that kid would have a sled of his own. I had to share mine with my brothers. They had it for downhill and I for uphill.

Mama made me a first-day-of-school pair of pants out of my sister Dora's gym bloomers. They almost made me a dropout at the age of six. I got home before lunchtime—much before—hid under the bed, and made it known that "I'm not going back to school. Kill me! I'm not going back."

"What's the matter?"

"You know what's the matter—the pants, that's what's the matter!"

"And what's the matter with the pants?"

"They're Dora's bloomers, that's what's the matter!"

"Who knows it's Dora's bloomers? Only you and me."

"Nobody knows, huh? So how come they keep chasing me out of the Boys' Room?"

Such maximal use of raw materials is possible only in a home in which ownership is relative. (The more relatives the less ownership.) We were taught that the good earth and all the things upon it were only on loan to us, that we had an obligation to divvy up everything with the needy—and who wasn't needy at some time or other?

45

We lived not only on borrowed time but on borrowed shoes, sweaters, coats.

"Why are you wearing my raincoat?"

"You wouldn't want me to get your suit wet, would you?"

In Mama's home nothing was embroidered "His" or "Hers." Mama had embroidered our minds with "It's not his and not hers, it's everybody's. But it would be very nice if you asked if you could have it for a while, thank you very much."

"Ma, should I start a fresh towel?" still runs through my mind. (Only Papa had that right, something like the medieval *droit du seigneur*.) When visiting people's homes I still cannot bring myself to use one of those nice clean guest towels. I look for an old one behind the door, and if I don't find it, I use either the inside of the shower curtain or the bottom of my host's bathrobe. My hands are clean and so is my conscience. "I didn't start a fresh towel, Ma."

I still wear my newest suit last, not first; otherwise I feel dressed to kill, a carry-over from "You're wearing your new suit? Mama'll kill you!"

My son Conrad later in life proved his ability as a conservationist. All of our family was very proud when *The New York Times* ran a picture story on the uniquely artistic home this young architect and his wife Isabella had created, rich in objets d'art, most of which he had picked up on the street, the beach, or out of the debris left when Coney Island's Steeplechase was torn down. He was one foot ahead of the bulldozers.

But as a child he had what to us was an unbelievable habit. He left food on his plate. This caused every known Levenson to look upon him with suspicion. I called my older brothers together (for dinner, naturally) in emergency session to try to recall where on our family tree there had been some nut who didn't lick his plate clean.

We all watched in horror as my unnatural son sat there beating prunes to death with the palm of his hand, straining Pablum through his teeth, strangling strands of spaghetti, squeezing cream puffs through his fists—"See the snakes, Mommy?" He killed our appetites too. My wife bought a book on the feeding problem. It made suggestions.

Suggestion: *Mealtime Must Be Happy*.

We danced for him. We sang for him. We put on a floor show three times daily and four on Sunday. Our performance made him happy but still not hungry.

Suggestion: *Mealtime Can Be Story-Telling Time*.

"Mary had a little . . ."—and the cereal went smack into his little ear as he made a sharp left turn from the spoon. "It's fleece was white as . . ."—up his nose. At parties Conrad recited those famous lines as he knew them: "Mary had a little spoon. Her fleece was white as farina."

Suggestion: *Offer Him His Favorite Foods*.

"Conrad, do you like spinach?"

Since his mouth was closed for the duration, he could only nod affirmatively. We figured that meant he liked spinach.

"Will you eat spinach?"

His head swiveled from left to right and back again. "Nope."

"Conrad, do you like eggs?"

Affirmative, mechanical up-and-down movement in the manner of a toy turtle, which we took to mean "Yes."

"Will you eat eggs?"

Back to west-east-east-west motion. "Nope."

We tried the numbers game. "Just take two spoonfuls. We'll count them together. Ready? One." (Into the mouth!) "One and a half." (Into the mouth!) "One and three quarters." (Into the mouth!) We could carry it to five decimal places, but he didn't swallow the trick or anything else.

We appealed to his altruism. If he didn't care to eat for himself, maybe he would eat for others. "A spoon for Uncle

Harry. And a spoon for Aunt Dora . . ." This game could also be played in a version known as the Train Ride. Like all kids, he loved trains. "We are all going on a train ride, and you are the train. Everybody on the train! Uncle Harry's getting on the train" (in went a spoonful of Uncle Harry); "Uncle Joe is getting on the train" (and he opened his mouth to let Uncle Joe on the train); "Hopalong Cassidy's getting on the train, and Ed Sullivan's getting on the train . . ." We were never sure how many passengers we could safely load onto the train without risking an accident. One day it happened. He held up his little hand like a trainman and announced: "Somebody better get off the train"—and they all did.

My mother-in-law took over his rehabilitation. She prepared a nice big bowl of chopped liver and onions smothered in love and chicken fat. She fed it to him, not with one of those cute little baby spoons but with a ladle. She told him he was a big lion, and that all lions lived on chopped liver; that's why they were so strong and roared a lot. He ate, roared, and belched through every opening in his body. To get him to drink, Grandma put a nipple on the ketchup bottle. He drank—anything, to douse the fire in his tummy.

No one ever had to tell us stories to interest us in food. (With our childhood appetites, if you had put sugar on a fly it would have tasted like a huckleberry.) We were told stories to distract us. One brother would say, "Look who came in." I would turn my head, and my meat balls would be gone. They would tell me I ate them, and I believed them.

When brother Bill's appendix kicked up and he was taken to the hospital in the middle of dinner, we ran after the ambulance shouting, "Bill! Bill! Who gets your strudel?"

Food was thrown in, not out. Each of us functioned like a garbage pail. Mama stepped on your foot, you opened your mouth, in went something, and you flipped your lid. (The only things that got thrown out were kids who threw things out.)

"There is no such thing as bad food," Mama used to say, "there are only spoiled children."

"Ma, I'm hungry."

"Smear a little chicken fat on a piece of bread."

"I don't like bread and chicken fat."

"If you don't like bread and chicken fat, you're not hungry. The children in China would be glad to have it."

When brother David first gazed on the immense dinosaur skeleton at the Museum of Natural History his reaction was: "Boy! What a soup Mama could make out of that!"

"Liver for the cat" was a common ruse. Everybody knew it, including the butcher.

"Mr. Butcher, the liver you threw into the order yesterday for the cat was not fresh."

"Did it make the cat sick?"

"Sick! He couldn't go to school for two days."

My elegant brother Mike made Mama's culinary resuscitations sound fancy by given them French names: hamburger accumulé, liver reclamé, dragout prolongué, beef retourné, onion refraîché, salmon rejuvenué, eggs renaissance, pâté continué, soupe toujours, and caviar jamais. Garlic, cabbage, peppers, and radishes repeated by themselves. (Papa had trouble finding something to bless in Mama's food which he had not already blessed on previous occasions.)

We were reared in a superstition that warned against leaving your tooth mark in a morsel of uneaten food. In some crime lab in the sky they would track the wastefulness back to your molars and punish you.

Today we are no longer superstitious. We have the best-fed garbage cans in the world, filled to overflowing with food that has been stabbed, cut, tasted, and rejected. We cut away the skin, the fat, the gristle, the bone. We are prosperous.

49

"Ma, the cheese smells."

"Throw it out, honey."

"Ma, the soda has no fizz."

"Start another bottle, baby."

"Ma, the banana has brown spots."

"Don't touch it; it could be diseased." (To us a banana was a black fruit with yellow spots.)

"Ma, this apple has pits."

"Spit them out, dear, they're not good for you." (We were told, "Eat them! You think apples grow on trees?")

"Don't eat the white," they now warn watermelon-eating kids. We were told, "Don't eat the green."

"Ma, my cookie fell on the floor."

"Take another, dear. It has germs now."

"Ma, the bread is moldy."

"Don't touch it. Moldy bread is bad for you." (Since when is penicillin bad for you?)

If an egg fell on the floor, Mama looked at it and said, "Oh, well. I'll bake a cake." She would run her thumb along the inside of the eggshell, scooping out everything down to and including the little membrane at the bottom. If a piece of candy fell off the table, it hardly ever reached the floor; the germs would have had to fight us for the candy. If it did get as far as the floor, we not only picked it up but kissed it and murmured something sacred before we ate it. It was not the germs we feared but God.

Our children know nothing about the art of licking. We lick-polished fingers, hands, plates, spoons, sleeves, ties—and none of these had to be our own.

I have seen kids these days take bites out of an ice cream cone. We never did that. We started by licking. After you had licked the ball of ice cream down to the rim of the cone, you inserted the mouth of the cone into your mouth and blew into it. This sent the now softened cream down into the lower half of the cone. You then bit the small tip at the lower end, making a tiny hole. Now you did not blow, but sucked a tiny drop at a time, holding it under your tongue without swallowing for as long as possible. When the cone and the ice cream gave out, you went back to licking your fingers, all ten, one at a time, slowly.

Jelly preserves were more often preserved from us rather than for us. "Don't touch the jelly; it's for company. Maybe somebody will drop in." In order to become company or somebody, we would have to visit somewhere else, somewhere where *they* were nobody and *we* could be somebody.

If we ran short of food for a visiting somebody, the code word came down the line—"F.H.B." (Family Hold Back). One day Uncle Louie and Aunt Lena and their brood of somebodies happened to be in the neighborhood at dinner time. Our combined eating potential now came to about sixteen manpower units. But we knew we could count on Mama's magic pot. No matter how many somebodies dropped in, Mama merely dipped her ladle into the bottomless pot and came up with endless amounts of rainy-day chicken legs.

Anyhow, on this rainy day either Mama had lost her magic touch or her pact with the chicken genie had run out, but she didn't have enough legs to go round. She saw the handwriting on the bottom of the pot: "Lady. You haven't a leg to stand on."

Mama called a meeting of her own flesh and blood, not to consult but to order: "Children, say you don't like chicken!"

The modern mother caught in a similar dilemma would probably run into some resistance: "What do you mean give up *my* chicken? It's *my* chicken. So if he's an uncle, so what? Who comes first? A child or an uncle?"

We offered no resistance. We even collaborated with the enemy.

"Have some chicken, Sammy."

"No, thank you. I don't like chicken . . . I hate chicken . . . I just ate chicken . . . I never eat chicken"—and the saliva ran out of my ears, down my chin, into my shirt, and onto my stomach.

When we got around to the dessert, Mama pulled a trick for which today the American Society for the Prevention of Cruelty to Children would march her off to jail. In the same calm, self-assured tone in which she had drafted us into the conspiracy she announced: "Now, all the children who refused to eat chicken don't get any dessert!"

I let the dessert go not only out of consideration for Mama but because of my faith in the covenant between Mama, the United States of America, and me, to the effect that "if you'll be a good boy, and you'll work hard, and suffer now, some day you'll get your true dessert." I was a good boy, and I did work, and suffered, and now that I can afford the dessert, the doctors won't let me have it. It's fattening. Where were the smart doctors with their appetite depressants when the saliva was running down my chin? Today I'm more hungry than ever, and there's no hope for a better tomorrow. I, who was taught to count my blessings, must now learn to count my calories instead.

I want my dessert. I've waited long enough.

For years now I have been pilloried by pills—yellow, blue, and gray. They either make me see double, so that I feel twice as full on half as much, or shut off the blood to my brain, paralyzing my eating arm. (The other arm has to be left flexible enough to pay the doctor.)

I found out that, like everybody else, I weigh less in the morning. I don't sleep nights waiting to rejoice at the dawn's early light. If I haven't lost enough, I go back to bed for an hour and try again.

I bought a bathroom scale. More problems. With my figure and my eyes, I can't see the numbers. If I bend over, the numbers go up. That's bad. My wife has to lie on the floor and call out numbers to me. When she isn't around, I use my son's binoculars. I discovered that if I move the bathroom scale to a room where the floor slants a little, I can lose weight without struggling.

I have become a pretty good cheat and an even better liar. I steal food from friends' plates on the assumption that since I didn't order it, it's not fattening. I pick up crumbs (pounds of) with the tip of my moistened index finger. (I create crumbs by accidentally crushing rolls with my elbow.) I eat my children's leftovers because "It's a shame to leave it." (That's how Mama got fat—from shame. It was a shame to leave this and a shame to leave that.)

I rationalized my failure to lose fat with fat lies. "I've got big bones"; "It's glandular"; "It's all water"; "I've always been heavy, so for me I'm not fat"; "If I just look at a cream puff I get fat" (so I eat without looking).

I avoid midnight snacks, as my doctor tells me. I go to bed hungry. Every night, all night, I dream of sumptuous testimonial dinners, banquets, and receptions in my honor. I eat and eat and eat. In the morning I feel full. I notice that pieces of quilt are missing, but I don't mention it to my doctor.

I morbidly stalk fat neighbors, expecting them to collapse the way the actuarial tables say they must. They don't, and I don't have the heart to tell them their days are numbered. They are such nice people. I meet them regularly at the funerals of skinny doctors.

I eat sandwiches without bread. I skip one meal a day—a procedure that has me eating lunch for breakfast, dinner for lunch, and the next day's breakfast in the evening. I have opened a calorie bank, adding calories to one meal to be withdrawn from the next. I run into debt. I doctor the books so that even I won't know. I devour rich foods to get them out of my sight so I won't be tempted to eat them later. I have even found myself swearing to get a picket sign and go on a hunger strike against dieting.

I have finally perfected the irreducible reducing formula. I have at last shed my dread of bread. You don't have to suffer. You like bread? Eat bread! You like potatoes? Eat potatoes! You like dessert? Eat dessert! Eat whatever you like. Just don't swallow.

IV

You Never Get the Dessert

If I had to do it all over again today, I couldn't afford it. I spent so many years of my life learning how to make ends meet. Now that I have the means, they have moved the ends farther apart. Like the racetrack rabbit pursuing but never catching the carrot, the cost of living has always been just ahead. The possible dream never catches up with the impossible price. When I earned thirty dollars a week the rent was forty; when I earned forty it went to sixty; when I got to sixty it was up to one hundred. It now takes ten times one's means to live within them. I used to buy birthday presents for what the accompanying card costs now.

The penny I saved for a rainy day has come upon bad days. Pennies lie around in desk drawers alongside rusty paper clips and dead rubber bands. They are even scorned by machines: "This machine does not take pennies." Neither do toll bridges, turnstiles, or panhandlers. Children give them to their fathers.

The truth is that pennies are hardly worth pinching. The only thing you can still get for a penny is your incorrect weight. "A penny for your thoughts" is now fifty dollars an hour with the psychoanalyst, for the very same thoughts. Penny banks sell for $1.80 and take only dimes. An apple a day costs more than calling the doctor. And if the doctor tells you you're sound as a dollar, you're really in trouble. The way things are going, the only thing I will have left for a rainy day is my arthritis.

But, thank God, I don't have to worry about rainy days any more. I can get an umbrella on credit. "Charge" is no longer a military term. Debt is no longer a shame; it's a sign of success. To be a credit to my family, my community, and my country today I need a credit card. Debt by choice rather than necessity is smart. Paying in cash is a sign of poverty. In a department store it is a disgrace. I still try to pay in cash, but there is always a scene at the cashier's desk. They send for managers and house detectives; they ring bells, wave papers in the air, talk on intercoms, gather a crowd. I'm glad that I don't get arrested.

"You'd like to pay in cash? You will need two references." To avoid public humiliation I have been forced to use credit cards. I am eligible. Anybody who has a good job, a bank account, and doesn't need credit is eligible. My credit is good. I can borrow on one credit card to cover the unpaid bills on another credit card. I can even buy credit-card insurance against loss of credit cards with a credit card.

There is a disturbing significance in the fact that the pictures of my family are being forced out of my bulging wallet by my credit cards. Who steals my purse steals my good name, and I get his bills.

I still believe in to each his own rather than to each his owe (the lay-awake plan), even in an era in which we are pressured to owe as you go, to eat now, drive now, get sick now, and pay later. The card-carrying American has more to live for than ever before: his house isn't paid for, his washing machine isn't paid for, his war isn't paid for. Industry invests fortunes in longevity research to make sure he will live long enough to finish all his easy payments. If you should fall behind in your payments, you won't be sent to jail. No. You can surrender the partially paid-for merchandise and retrieve it on the same day with an easy down payment plus the payment of penalties for the nonpayment of previous penalties plus interest charges. "Just sign here. Your credit is good."

My outstanding debt, one that I shall never be able to repay in full, is for the freedom I have had to work, to earn, and to pay for what I need.

❀ ❀ ❀

Life collects its taxes in one form or another.

When I was a teacher, working for the government, I didn't earn much, but I had security. What I didn't realize when I gave up my steady job to seek my fortune was that the more fortunate I would be, the more I'd be working for the same government, without the security, but steady.

I owed it to myself to do well, but I didn't know I was going to owe it all to the government. Uncle Sam pinches my cheek even harder than Uncle Louie did. "Yesh, Uncle Sham. I work hard, fank you, Uncle Sham. Me goo boy." And for being a good boy and working hard I give *him* money.

Now, if I give my uncle such a generous allowance every year, don't I have the right (like Papa) to ask, "What are you gonna do with the money?" Look, dear uncle, you try to live on your income, and I'll try to live on mine.

❀ ❀ ❀

My first encounter with the Internal Revenue Service (at that time called the Bureau of Internal Revenue) occurred

57

long before I became one of their clients. I was in college at the time.

A man from the government came to Papa's tailor shop to investigate him. Washington could not believe that a man with so many kids could live on so little. We knew that Papa had not evaded the income tax; he and the income had evaded each other. He was the head of a nonprofit organization.

I saw poor Papa's face go white. I understood. He had never lost his fear of "Government," even the U.S. government, which in his mind still represented Them, not Us. His memory went back to when government meant czarist officers, cossacks and pogroms. Papers and investigations meant trouble. This man in his dark-blue suit (Papa could recognize government cloth) carrying papers was enough to make Papa quiver. But I was not afraid, not me. This was *my* government.

The government man politely inquired whether he could ask a few questions. Seeing Papa in his skullcap, he turned to me: "Does your father speak English?" I answered simply that I had better act as an interpreter. Papa knew enough English to get along, but he had no intention of getting along with this man. There was no point in explaining Papa's ethnic resistance to giving up his ways for "their" ways. "Let *them* learn Yiddish! How could anybody live in this country so many years and not know Yiddish!"

I had tried to teach Papa to spell. It was a strictly business deal, a nickel a week. We started off fine. No problems. The Hebrew and English alphabets were about the same: *a, b, c— aleph, beth, gimel.* "*They* took *our* alphabet," Papa said in amazement, and off he went to spell "cat," "bat," "rat," "hat" after the first lesson.

The trouble started with "cook," "book," "look." "Why do *they* need two *o*'s?" I needed those nickels, so I assured him "they" were wrong, but that's the way it was. When we got to "night," "light," "bright," Papa suspected me of stretching the words to prolong the lessons. Besides, he refused to pay for letters he didn't pronounce. At "borough" he threw up his hands in disgust. "I see *they* don't want me to learn! Either *they* spell it b-o-r-o or you can tell *them* I'll get along without *their* crazy language." They wouldn't take his advice, so he quit.

There was a secondary anger in Papa that was directed not against "them" as government but against "them" as the entire industrial civilization. Papa had been trained from the age of six to be a master craftsman in the old guild system. By the time he got to America he was a superb artist with a needle; but what was needed here was not men who could turn out the work good, but fast. "They" had destroyed his pride in his workmanship. To Papa this was an attack on his person.

So the day that man came to Papa's shop I knew right away the government was in trouble. In the old country Papa had had no alternative but to answer questions. In America he could refuse.

The government opened its case with "How much does your father earn a week?"

I knew the answer, if not the exact words. Papa never even told Mama. He was going to tell this stranger? Why does *he* have to know how this poor Jew is doing? What business was it of *his*? I translated the question into Yiddish, and got an answer in Yiddish, which I retranslated into English for the government.

"My father says that his worst enemies should earn what he earns."

The investigator studied his standard answer sheets, but obviously found nothing remotely resembling "Enemies, worst."

He tried again.

"Ask your father how much rent he pays."

I went through the process of translation again, with this result: "My father says the landlord should have so many boils on his neck how much too much he pays."

I could see the beads of sweat collecting on the government's forehead. He stepped outside, studied the store window, checked the number on the door, obviously wondering whether he was in the right place. He didn't even look at his answer sheets again.

"Just one more question, son. Ask your father who owned this store before him."

"Papa, the man wants to know who owned this store before you."

"Tell him some other poor shnook with a house full of loafers."

By the time I turned around to deliver the translation the G-man was heading for the door mumbling in what sounded like Yiddish. He didn't look sane to me, but Papa never looked better. He was beaming. He had defended the Bill of Rights.

"It's a good country," Papa said in perfect English.

V

Auto Biography

❀ ❀ ❀

I know that Miss McGregor Miss McGregor (the same Miss McGregor Miss McGregor who had introduced me to banking) intended only to broaden our horizons when she showed the entire school that enticing travelogue, the one that sent Albert and me home with a burning passion to see the world. To this day we refer to what happened to us as the "bus accident." It was a traumatic affair, which proved two things: one, that the shape of the world was indeed round; and two, that considering the shape we were in, we couldn't afford to see the world, no matter what shape it was in.

We had seen sight-seeing buses on the streets. We had also seen posters that said, "See America First." We were willing to start even more modestly. "Hey, Al. How about we start with New York?"

We saved penny upon penny, each night measuring the growing pile of pennies, hoping to see them and us rising high enough to make it over the rooftops to the world out

61

there. Thirty-two cents to go . . . twenty-eight cents to go . . . ten cents to go . . . Over the top! We kept the entire project a secret from our parents, who would have found a more "sensible" use for our fifty cents. (Parents always have to be "sensible.") They probably would have called us "crazy or something" and confiscated the money. (What's so sensible about that?)

On Sight-seeing Day we walked to Times Square, each of us loaded down with fifty pennies. We waited in line with people so rich they had the whole fare in one coin. We took seats behind each other so we could each have a window. When the motor started we held our breath. "The longest journey begins with but a single step." This was ours. I shall never know to what extent that experience has affected our emotional lives. I know only that the first sight the sight-seeing bus took us to see was our own block.

If you don't count the time Albert was delivered to the hospital in the vegetable truck that hit him (which he continues to claim as a ride), it would be a long time before either of us would venture out into the world again in a motor vehicle.

I interpreted the fiasco of the sight-seeing bus as a sign that I had reached beyond my grasp, beyond what life intended for me at that time. "Like they say," Albert said, "you can't put the bus before the cart." I would have to travel block by block and pay the toll at each corner. Today the block; to-morrow the world. Some day I would own a car of my own; then I would see the world—even if it cost a dollar.

In the meantime there were other places I could visit, close by, but still outside of my home—like our fire escape. It served mainly as an open-air storage bin for gallon jugs of benzine, kerosene, naphtha, and turpentine. In case of fire it was the most dangerous place in the world to be. We put up a sign on the fire escape: *In case of fire, run into the house.*

Or we could travel six flights to the roof (Tar Beach),

where on hot Sunday afternoons men, women, children, and the heat would gather. If by evening the heat did not subside, up would come the mattresses. Each family would pick a section of gravel the size of a double bed, and stretch out to be tarred and feathered for the night.

The roof offered me my first view of space, glorious space. As night descended I watched God's lights go on. Papa and I saw it differently. My eyes looked up and explored the heavens; Papa's looked down and deplored the earth.

"Papa, do you know how fast light travels?"

"All I know is it gets here too early in the morning."

"Papa, you know the difference between lightning and electricity?"

"From lightning you don't get bills."

"Papa, they say that some day the world is gonna come to an end."

"We'll get along without it."

"Papa, there's a falling star. Make a wish."

"I wish you'd stop bothering me."

On hot Fridays I got as far as the Ninety-second Street YMHA. Friday mornings they let in hundreds of us kids for free (they were draining the pool anyhow). As the water in the pool got lower we swam faster and faster, down to the last drop. To this day I can swim better over bodies than over water, especially if I have a piece of soap in my hand. Mama always said, "Take soap."

I could also sneak off to the nearby East River for b.a. swimming (without soap or consent). For swimming in the East River you had to use a special stroke. You propelled yourself forward by kicking your feet, using your hands somewhat like an ice cutter to part the flowing sewage ahead of you. When I got back home I would stand there, the foul-smelling bilge still trickling from my hair, swearing to Mama that I had been to the library.

"The library?" Mama sniffed. "What kind of books were you reading?"

At least once each summer we kids went off on a hike, but never without strong opposition from Mama. When it came to the open road Mama had a closed mind. Anything beyond our immediate neighborhood was wilderness. Once she set foot out of the house she lost her bearings. When she did venture out she traveled by landmarks.

For a visit to Aunt Bessie she got on the trolley at our corner and got off at a corner where there was a furniture store with a brown bed in the window. The road to Aunt Naomi passed two churches, one movie house, one large school, one small school, and a tailor shop.

Sometimes, just to make sure, she would ask the conductor questions like "This is the second school?" or "Where do the tracks go round and round and come out under an elevator?"

She would often lose patience, get off the trolley, and go in search of two churches, which she somehow always found. After a while she gave up the trolley completely, and would walk from our house, following the tracks past two churches, one movie house, one large school, one small school, and a tailor shop to Aunt Naomi's house. When the tailor moved away she wound up in the trolley yard.

Her method of dissuading us from venturing out into the unknown was to make the entire project appear ridiculous.

"You're going on a what?"

"We're going on a hike."

"What's a hike?" Mama would ask.

When we started to explain it, the whole idea did in fact become ludicrous.

"We go walking, Ma."

"Walking? For that you have to leave home? What's the matter with walking right here? You walk; I'll watch."

"You don't understand, Ma. We take lunch along."

"I'll give you lunch here, and you can march right around the table"—and she would start singing a march, clapping her hands rhythmically.

"Ma, we climb mountains in the woods."

She couldn't understand why it was so much more enjoyable to fall off a mountain than off a fire escape.

"And how about the wild animals in the woods?"

"Wild animals? What kind of wild animals?"

"A bear, for instance. A bear could eat you up."

"Ma, bears don't eat little children."

"Okay, so he won't eat you, but he could take a bite and spit out! I'm telling you now, if a wild animal eats you up, don't come running to me. And who's going with you?"

"Well, there's Georgie . . ."

"Georgie! Not him! He's a real wild animal!" She then went on to list all the conditions for the trip. "And remember one thing, don't tear your pants; and remember one thing, don't eat wild berries and bring me home the cramps; and remember one thing, don't tell me tomorrow morning that you're too tired to go to school; and remember one thing, wear rubbers, a sweater, warm underwear, and an umbrella, and a hat; and remember one thing, if you should get lost in the jungle, call up so I'll know you're all right. And don't dare come home without color in your cheeks. I wish I was young and free like you. Take soap."

Since the consent was specifically granted for the next day only, that night none of us slept. There was always a chance that it might rain. Brother Albert stayed at the crystal set all night like a ship's radio operator with his earphones on, listening to weather bulletins and repeating them aloud for the rest of us. "It's clearing in Nebraska. Hot air masses coming up from the Gulf. They say it's good for planting alfalfa. Storm warning off the coast of Newfoundland. It's drizzling in Montreal."

At 6:00 A.M. we were ready for Operation Hike, rain or shine, but we had to wait for Papa to get up. We didn't need his permission, but we did need his blanket.

Into the valley of Central Park marched the six hundred bowed down with knapsacks, flashlights, a Cracker Jack box compass-mirror (so you could tell not only where you were lost but who was lost), a thermos bottle (semi-automatic—you had to fill it, but it emptied by itself), and an axe. Onward! Forward! Upward! "Ours not to reason why." Philip was always the leader. He was the one to get lost first. Jerry was the lookout. He would yell, "Look out!" and fall off a cliff. None of us knew how long we were supposed to march. We went on because we wouldn't know what to do if we stopped. One brave coward finally spoke up. "I can't go on any more. The heat is killing me. Let's start the fire here."

No hike was complete without Georgie and his Uncle Bernie's World War I bugle. This kid had lungs like a vacuum cleaner. With him outside the walls of Jericho, they could have sent the rest of the army home. He used to stand on a hill and let go a blast that had the Staten Island ferries running into each other.

Lunch, naturally, was packed in a shoe box—sandwiches, fruit, cheese, and napkins—all squashed together neatly. The lid would open by itself every twenty minutes for air.

It happened every time, the Miracle of the Sandwiches. One kid always got a brilliant idea. "Hey, I got a brilliant idea. I'm tired of my mother's sandwiches. Let's everybody exchange sandwiches." All the kids exchanged sandwiches, and miraculously we all ended up with salami.

Albert was the true nature lover. "You know, you can learn a lot about human nature from the ants," he always said as he lifted up rock after rock to study his favorite insects. And he was right. While he was studying the ants someone swiped his apple.

We came home with color in our cheeks—green. To make

sure we could go again, we didn't forget Mama. We brought her a bouquet. She took one whiff and broke out in red blotches. Papa yelled but didn't lay a hand on us. He was afraid it was catching.

Sometimes Papa went out with us, but not on "foolishness" like a hike.

At the end of a sweat-shop week, on a meager supply of strength, money, shoe leather, and patience, Papa tried to expose us to the better things in life by taking us on a trip to the museum, for example.

As usual, we walked, and as usual, Mama made us take sandwiches. We carried more provisions than the expeditions that had brought back the mummies. Papa, the guide, marched on ahead, and we of the children's safari trailed after him. "Look, kids. If you're going to stop and look at everything you're not going to see nothing." We covered some four thousand years of civilization in twenty minutes.

We had been warned to whisper. That wasn't easy for kids who were in the habit of shouting to each other from rooftops. Whispering made us hoarse.

Papa tried to rush us past the naked statues to avoid embarrassing us and himself. We looked at each other knowingly and tried to giggle in a whisper. Nakedness, Papa explained, was all right here because it was "from long ago."

Our good behavior broke down only when brother Bill took a drink from a Greek fountain and was grabbed by a guard. We tried so hard to stifle our laughter we got hysterical. The combination of water in the nose and fear in the heart gave Bill the hiccups, the echoes of which resounded and multiplied through the marble galleries till it sounded like a pack of hunting dogs. We were escorted out by a guard who suggested that Papa take us to the zoo. Since the zoo was only a few blocks from the museum, and since we already had sandwiches, and since one such outing for Papa was easier than two, Papa took us to see "the other wild animals."

We stationed ourselves in front of the lion's den and waited for the king of beasts to become ferocious. Apparently we and he had plenty of time. Every fifteen minutes he slowly raised one bloodshot eyelid to see if we were still there, then went back to sleep—no roars, no growls, a little belching perhaps. "Keep moving," Papa growled. We could count on him.

The caged gorilla looked no more dangerous than an unkempt boarder hiding in his room to avoid meeting his landlady. We had seen him before.

The elephant stood in the doorway of his quarters exposing only his hindquarters to the public, swaying just a bit to let us know that he knew what he was doing, while other, obviously wealthy, kids (their jackets matched their pants) threw expensive peanuts at his noneating end.

No bird or beast lived up to its reputation or our expectation. The parrots stood on their perches, their heads cocked, listening to us repeating "Polly wants a cracker"; the skunks didn't stink; the hyenas didn't laugh; the cheetahs didn't cheet; the wolf looked sheepish; the wild boar looked bored; the gazelle limped; the polar bear was having a hot lunch; the lizard was eating ants off the anteater; the boa constrictor was crushing a banana; and the owl just didn't give a hoot. The angriest creatures were in the building marked *Men,* and Papa was the angriest of all.

"Next time I take you any place I'm gonna leave you home."

❁ ❁ ❁

The Roaring Twenties didn't reach our block till the early thirties.

Hikes, museums, and zoos were all right for boys, but the young men on the block, including brothers Bill and Mike, felt a raging need to roar along. You couldn't roar without a

68

car, so they pooled their funds, and for twenty dollars picked up a twelve-cylinder, eight-seater, leather-upholstered funeral Packard. The horn emitted a death rattle, and the draped windows were always at half-mast. When it came down our street for the first time, dogs who normally barked at anything in motion stood in silent respect. It had headlights the size of bank clocks, and a trunk large enough to hold two spare tires and one coffin. When it idled it shook like an animal coming out of water.

To take the curse off its lugubrious past, they painted it over with hotcha slogans proclaiming their joy to the world: "Coney Island or Bust," "Oh, you kid!" "Night Riders," "Capacity 8 Gals," "The Biggest Milk Shaker in Town," "23 Skidoo." They would pull up to a gas station at a screaming thirty miles an hour and yell, "One gallon and lots of free air."

Each Saturday night they tried for Coney Island and busted. At 2:00 A.M. you could see the flaming youths pushing their burned-out car back into the block to the roaring of their parents, who called the cream of our young manhood "rotten bums," slapped their "rotten faces," and spat on their "rotten car."

❀ ❀ ❀

I was about twenty-five before I could afford a car or a wife, but not yet a car and a wife. Either license cost about the same, so I chose a wife. Together we found ways of getting rides without owning a car. The real-estate developers offered young couples free rides to see "Your Dream House on Long Island." Every Sunday we allowed ourselves to be driven to another dream house with a hobby room in the basement. For several years our Sunday hobby was looking at hobby rooms in dream houses.

Teaching school and dashing about doing performances at the same time finally made a car a necessity, but it was not yet to be. Man proposes; God disposes. The stork was racing the car to our house, and the bird came in first. We gladly kept the boy, and sadly let the dream car idle for a while. You can't have everything. We converted our car fund into fuel, oil, and seat covers for our first runabout, whom we named Conrad. (I was tempted to call him Ford.)

It took about three years more before we could afford both kid and car. I went by train to Allentown, Pennsylvania, to drive back a "practically new" secondhand car that had been "driven by a little old lady only to church and back." I had come for my reward. All speed ahead now to make up for the years and years of waiting!

I started for home. The world was mine, but the road sure wasn't! That little old lady in Allentown was apparently doing a thriving business. Sam Levenson and all his American-Irish-Italian-Polish-Hungarian-Ukrainian-German counterparts were reaping their rewards at the same moment. We had all been mobilized simultaneously. Upward mobility had worked. Horizontal mobility was another story. Off I went for about four feet, right up to the rear of the car ahead.

There I was, suspended in time and space, a victim of the counterpull of dream and reality, motion and inertia, power and powerlessness, at a dead standstill in bumper-to-bumper forced togetherness on the royal road to nowhere, listening to the restive neighing of three hundred gasoline-fed horses under the hood and radio bulletins from an overhead helicopter announcing to the world out there that I was "moving along at a brisk pace."

I got home at about 3:00 A.M., left the car in front of the house, and staggered into bed, not to sleep, but to wait for the sunrise of our new life. Soon everybody would be up, and together we would celebrate. In the morning we got dressed in our holiday clothes and went out to meet our car. It was there, and we were "in." We were finally full-fledged citizens. We not only had our very own car but our very own brand new U.S. government-approved parking ticket. My education as a motorist had begun.

I had never before read those traffic signs posted on the block. Now I had to. They looked like blowups of the small print on an insurance policy, except that they were printed vertically:

No Parking
This Side
2 to 4
6 to 8
8 to 10
Tues.–Thurs.–Sat.
Except
Alt. Mon.–Wed.–Fri.
3 to 5
7 to 9
11 to 12
Mon.–Thurs.–Sun.
Except Holidays
Here to Corner
No Standing
No Loading
No Unloading

The nice policeman on the block didn't understand the signs any better than I did. "Don't ask me, Mac. We don't write the signs; we just write the tickets."

I also had to learn about parking meters. (We almost got parking meters on our block, but the truck delivering them couldn't find a place to park.) Paying the dime didn't bother me, but stopping strangers on the street to ask for change made me feel like a panhandler. I had never begged on the street even in my poorest days. Going into stores to ask for change without buying something seemed like an imposition, so I always ended up buying something that cost seventy-five cents in order to get a dime for the meter.

The dream of a parking place of my own began to replace the dream of a car of my own. I soon learned that I had to get out of bed early enough to move my car to the other side of the street, and, if I was away, to call home at noon to ask my wife to move the car back to our side of the street. I began to understand why a thirty-hour work week was necessary. I had to quit work early enough to allow myself an extra half hour to dig up a decent resting place for my car. There weren't any, not even in front of a hydrant.

However, all disadvantages, I believed, would be outweighed by the golden opportunity my car would give me to broaden my children's horizons far beyond what Papa had been able to do for me. I would be able to take my family everywhere. Papa was B.C.—before car; I was A.C.—after car.

Every Sunday morning we arranged ourselves in the car: one mommy and one daddy in the front seat, two children (Conrad and Emily, our second car), Grandma and Grandpa (my wife's parents), and Aunt Sarah in the back seat; or one mommy, one daddy, and one child in the front, and another child and Grandma and Grandpa and Aunt Sarah in the back; or any other possible combination for road-testing the love of those we love the best.

Once we were all in our places we closed all the windows and set out in search of fresh air. Any open window created a draft that hit Grandma's neck and Grandpa's feet. "We'll get to the fresh air soon. In the meantime you can watch the fresh air through the windows. Don't fight, children. Children, don't fight. Children! It doesn't matter who sits near which window. Conrad had this window last Sunday? You want this window this Sunday? You want the front window? Okay, Emily, ask Conrad nicely if he'll change with you. Who is what? Emily is seasick? Not on the blanket! Breathe into a brown-paper bag, Emily. Not the one with the sandwiches in it! Children, don't fight! I can't see in the mirror if you jump around. We forgot what? Emily forgot her little pink blanket? We are not going back!"

I knew the psychological risk of depriving Emily of her little pink blanket, the one she always dragged with her through the street, through the park, through sandboxes, through her tonsil operation, the one whose color she could feel in the dark of night. "That's not the pink one; that's the yellow one!" I had come to visualize her at her wedding all in white, her little pink blanket trailing after her down the aisle. Who ever heard of a bride without a little pink blanket? We went back for the blanket.

We started out again. "Look how close that maniac is driving ahead of me. Children, don't. Don't, children. Conrad threw the money into the toll machine last time? You wanna throw this time? Okay, but this time watch what you're doing." (On the hottest day of the previous year Emily had dropped a ball of vanilla ice cream into the hand of the toll collector, who promptly went into shock.)

"How much is the toll? Twenty-five? Thirty-five? Fifty? Wait! I have to work my way into the Exact Change Lane. You don't have the exact change? Somebody, come up with exact change! I'm stuck in the Exact Change Lane! I can't find my pocket! Okay, Emily, throw! You threw what? Twenty-five pennies? You missed? You get out and pick them up! Why are those sirens blowing? The cop said to go ahead?"

"You can't, Daddy, not until the light says 'Thank you.'"

"I'm going through. Jail must be such a nice quiet place!"

"Grandma has to go on the potty."

"Hurray! Let's pull over."

One Sunday we left the car at the pier and took the boat ride up the Hudson to Indian Point. We spent the first hour of our inland-waters cruise sliding about damp decks looking for a dry place to sit down. On the sunny side of the boat the seats were dry but the wind blew too hard. Emily was allergic to wind, Grandma to sun, and Grandpa felt a draft. Up front you got the spray in your face. In the back the spray in your face was mixed with soot. So we all settled down inside to watch the beautiful shoreline through portholes.

At Indian Point the children spent most of the day going to the toilet, then replenishing themselves with water from the public drinking fountain so they could return to the toilet.

When we finally got back to our car it was about six in the evening. The sun was still shining, and I was enjoying an inner glow of satisfaction from having been able to enrich the childhood experiences of my children. Still a teacher at heart, I said to everybody, "We're not far from my old block. I'd love you kids to see it." We got there just as twilight was descending on the tenements. We could barely make it through the street for the dozens of kids weaving around the car. On the stoops and sidewalks sat their parents on chairs, fruit boxes, milk cans. My emotions got all mixed up. I was of it, but not in it. I had left it for greener pastures. Maybe it was the position of the sun, maybe the long trip up the Hudson, but the block looked very green to me. I certainly didn't expect my children to see it that way. I thought I was trying to show them how good they had it, when Emily piped up with "Let me out. I wanna play with these kids." Within ten minutes she was skipping rope to Spanish rhymes. Ten minutes after that she was lost. When we found her she didn't want to go home. "Please, Daddy, I'm having so much fun." I gave her ten minutes more, after which she didn't ask to stay a while longer. No. Now it was "Let's move here!"

She had tears in her eyes and I in mine. The years began to spin backward, and I became my own father. "Next time I take you kids any place I'm gonna leave you home!"

One trip led to another. While we did not steal to support the habit, we did succumb to the escape it provided. I was not sure whether we were driving the car or it was driving us. The day Conrad announced, "I'm running away from home —who's gonna drive me?" I knew we were hooked.

Every car, to an extent we don't always care to admit, is a getaway car. The American success formula is first to get a home of your own, then to get a car of your own so you don't have to stay in that home of your own. Home, sweet home becomes the place where some of the family waits for the others to come back with the car so that *they* can take the car and go.

We were still to take the giant step forward that started with that single step into the sight-seeing bus. I convinced Esther that we should take a trip to Europe. After our honeymoon there were years during which our children had to get the measles, go to camp, break legs, run away, get lost, get found, grow up, get brassieres, get sports jackets, love their parents, hate their parents, bring home boys and girls, lock themselves in their rooms, and see the country. As for us, we waited and saved, and thirty years later we bought our first plane tickets to Paris.

To get to the new horizons we had to leave the old ones behind. Before turning toward Europe the plane made a sweeping review of the landmarks of Sammy's odyssey: tenements, fire escapes, rooftops, Times Square, East River, Hudson River, Coney Island, and finally the Atlantic Ocean. "Hey, look at those expanding horizons!" In eight hours we were in Paris, but our luggage was in New York, along with some poignant memories of our step-by-step pursuit of happiness. Perhaps much of the happiness had been in the pursuit. Or as my Uncle Benny always said, "It's not the sugar that makes the tea sweet, but the stirring."

VI
Frank Lloyd Wrong

❀ ❀ ❀

The morning after I got my own TV show I was petitioned by my friends and relatives to the effect that since I was now a "celebrity," and since the Levensons (previously known as Sam and Esther) were going to be entertaining "important people" (not persons, but "personalities"), and since the aforementioned friends and relatives wanted to share in my success . . . we must redo our apartment in order to avoid embarrassing *them*. Success oblige.

We had been so busy building a life and a suitable world to live it in that we had never thought of decorating. We never felt that our home needed cosmetics. Since we had no one to live up to but ourselves, our possessions had reflected our interiors. To us interior decorating meant polishing and refining our inner selves. Accumulating ornaments seemed like exterior rather than interior decorating. We kidded ourselves about our less than distinguished décor, calling it inferior decorating, Frank Lloyd Wrong, or Rank Lloyd Fright.

When success moved in with us we still had window shades

that flipped up madly in the middle of the night and had to be rewound with the prongs of a fork; guillotine windows that came down on your neck if you stuck your head out below; an integrated upright piano (the black and white keys stuck together in fair weather or foul); wall-to-wall bookshelves; Van Gogh prints that had been razor-cut from old magazines; diplomas framed in genuine Woolworth bamboo; an overwound victrola that made Caruso sound like Lily Pons and Lily Pons like bird imitations; and a couch upholstered in itchy mohair. Our classy-conscious friends recommended an interior decorator with a French accent and Italian pants who started us on the road to gracious living. Looking at furniture was our first giant social step forward. Our decorator thought perhaps we would like a tropical settee made of bleached bones upholstered in white fur for people who might not be satisfied with just skin and bones. We were warned that it could shed in the summer and had to be reupholstered by a veterinarian. (It was ideal for a home where the buffaloes roam, but for us . . .)

He urged us to keep up with the times by scouting around for something new in antiques. (Back to leftovers again.) They had to be at least one hundred years old to be "in." My mother-in-law didn't qualify. People do not become more valuable with age. Now, if she were a spinning wheel, or an apothecary jar, or a cobbler's bench, or a mortar and pestle, or a snuff box, or a wagon-wheel chandelier, or a Confederate drum, or an old milk-can umbrella stand, thousands of sophisticated homemakers would be bidding for her at auction sales.

As was to be expected, Grandma's unsolicited comments about the antiques did not endear her to the decorator: "A chair just like this one I threw out twenty years ago in better condition. . . . This they call a jardiniere? We used to call it a chamber pot. . . . Louis the Fourteenth couldn't afford an up-to-date bureau?"

We compromised. "Let's just buy a few new pieces, which our children will turn into antiques within one year."

We admitted to the decorator that squares like ourselves would never fit into round beds, nor were we interested in conversation pieces (we made our own conversation), or in reclining chairs (we were not used to talking to our feet), but we would like a new couch. This he got for us, along with the compulsory chintz slip covers, which he insisted we needed to protect the new fabric from fading, and compulsory plastic covers to slip over the slip covers to protect the slip covers from fading, even though the sunlight was blacked out by heavy drapes backed by heavy curtains backed by heavy Venetian blinds. We were back in the Dark Ages. Under no condition were we ever to expose our couch to the light of the sun, the moon, or the sight of man. We have not seen that beautiful fabric since the day it came.

The system of pulleys and ropes that controlled the drapes was too complicated for me. You had to be a union stagehand to work them. No matter which rope I yanked, the drapes closed. The curtains had their own set of gears, which operated in the opposite direction. The Venetian blinds had their private hoists and tackles. The old guillotine window no longer went up or down; the decorator put an organ-grinder's crank on it which made it open outward. The crank came off in my hand the first time I tried it, and the window remained permanently fixed in the open position.

We and the decorator parted company over his ideas for painting the rooms. It is a good thing that when God created the rainbow He didn't consult a decorator or He would still be picking colors.

For the living room we thought we'd like blue.

"Oh, blue?" said he spreading thirty volumes of blue samples on the floor. I had heard of true blue and blue with envy. I was now to meet ice blue, robin's-egg blue, navy blue, American navy blue, Japanese navy blue . . .

"Did you say gray?" I didn't, but he did. Horizon gray? Tool gray? Oyster gray? Cloister gray?

I came up with a few ideas of my own. For the kitchen tomato red, Pablum white, or prune with a dash of sour cream. For the bathroom maybe seaflush or potpourri, and for the baby's room perhaps sweet pea or dewkist. He not only liked my ideas, he came up with swatches.

We asked whether we could think it over for a while, like a year or five. We paid the ransom and bolted the door behind him.

We had to admit that we needed painting badly, but we were afraid to start up again with experts. Wasn't there somewhere a plain old-fashioned painter? It was then that I remembered Markowitz the painter, the man who used to paint Mama's apartment. True, he did not do it often, but the memory of his presence lingered on long after his colors had faded. The impression he made on our family was indelible.

As one waits for other legendary figures who are coming to fulfill some ancient promise made to man, Mama waited for this figure in white from the land of the landlord, as promised.

Mama made elaborate preparations for his coming—"not before Monday." The dishes were packed in barrels along with towels, tablecloths, underwear, and other things we could do without for a while. Monday came reliably, and Tuesday, and Wednesday, but not Markowitz. On Thursday he arrived, planted an opened can of turpentine in the middle of the floor, and said, "Like I said, Monday—not before."

Tuesday morning at 6:00 A.M. he shook Mama in bed and whispered, "You want I should paint the kitchen set too?" Mama woke with a scream, not knowing whether to run for the landlord, the police, the rabbi, or a dream interpreter.

By breakfast time the bedroom looked like a hastily improvised bomb shelter. Papa, protecting himself with an old

79

raincoat over his head and shoulders, looked like a captured German general. "The scaffold is too good for such painters," he grumbled.

Markowitz moved in with us for the duration—"our sleep-in painter," brother Mike called him. He smeared and talked, and talked, and talked.

"You're lucky, Mrs. Levenson, you have such a nice family. I had three. I lost one. She would have been as old as your Dora." By now he knew our names, which of us was good, which bad, which working, which studying. He would pick a photograph off the piano. "A nice face. He's not married? I have a girl for him. I think I smell coffee." He always thought he smelled coffee. "I wouldn't mind a coffee."

Over coffee he would reveal more of his past. "I didn't listen. I should have gone to school. I should have been a doctor. Blood is like music to me. Last week I painted a doctor's office. I worked overtime on my own time just to listen. Iodine, Argyrol, that's for me, not paint. Maybe I'm really like a doctor, anyhow. You take a sick apartment, and you fix all the cracks and patch it up and paint it up, and it's healthy again. Maybe God knows what He's doing, but I tell you something, Mrs. Levenson, when you say yellow for the bedroom you don't know what you're doing. For bedrooms there's only one color, ivory. Believe me, the best, the most practical, is ivory. The Park Avenue doctor's wife, she took ivory. I'll tell you what—ivory with a touch of yellow."

The painting took about one week. Getting back to normal took six months.

The windows were glued to the frames. Hammering the window frames only chipped off the fresh paint. It was wiser to wait till winter, when the frames would contract by themselves.

Rigor mortis had already set in on the door locks. The knobs spun around like pinwheels, but the tongues wouldn't come out. Some doors had swelled up and wouldn't close;

others had closed permanently and wouldn't open, sealing off closets and rooms like Egyptian tombs. Who knows what (or who) was left in them?

The kitchen table legs were glued to the floor. Four kids got under the table and, using their shoulders for leverage, jolted the table into the air, leaving four holes in the linoleum.

Markowitz had used a special paint for the toilet seat, which, he said, would dry in two hours. For weeks afterwards when one of us rose from the seat, part of him stayed behind.

The dining room set was so full of paint specks that it was easier to paint the chairs and table the same color as the specks than to try to remove them.

The piano solved its own problem, and it worked out all right: the black keys were now white and the white keys black—and if it was okay with them, it was okay with us.

In the end it turned out that Markowitz had been right in the first place. Everything was now ivory, except for Mama's hair, which was now a nice shade of gray.

So we remembered unforgettable Markowitz. Was he still alive? Maybe he could do our place. We searched him out. He was alive and well and living in the old neighborhood.

We rang his bell.

"You never forget Markowitz!" he proclaimed. He was available, but "not before Monday." We packed our barrels and waited. He arrived on Tuesday. "I think I smell coffee."

He did a complete repeat performance for us, including glued windows, jammed door locks, holes in the linoleum, white keys black, black keys white . . .

"There's only one Markowitz," he said as we paid him. "But I'll tell you the truth, if you wouldn't be angry, Mr. Levenson, a man in your position, you should get a decorator. I'll send you my son. He's an Interior Designer."

81

VII

The Men in Mama's Life

❀ ❀ ❀

Markowitz was one of a vanishing breed we called "the men in Mama's life." I can't remember their names now, but I hardly knew them then. I didn't have to. Their identifications were simple: the grocery man, the laundry man, the chicken man, the seltzer man, the fruit man, the candy-store man, the fish man, the herring man, the ice man, the pickle man, the egg man, the drugstore man, the shoestore man, the milk man. Each was a man (like Papa), with a wife (like Mama), and children (like us), and trouble (like ours)—a man for all seasons.

Mr. Man ran the kind of place to which any mama could safely send any kid alone. I was one of those kid couriers who arrived all day long by sneaker, by tricycle, or by fruit-box skooter to proclaim, "My mudder says she wants . . ." The emissary would then recite his message, either word for word from memory exactly as Her Majesty His Mother had told it to him, or read it (aloud with expression) from a scroll rolled up in his hand.

"My mudder says she wants meat for the cat. She says to make it lean. My fodder don't like fat."

"My mudder says she wants for ten cents cockroach powder. She says I shouldn't tell you what we need it for."

"My mudder says she wants for five cents animal crackers. She says, if you don't mind, you should please take out the pigs."

"My mudder says she wants change for a dollar. She says the dollar she'll give you Monday."

I loved going to the bakery. All the years that have passed since I carried Mama's messages there have not dissipated the memory of the living and loving aroma of fresh-baked bread which caressed the taste buds in my eyes, ears, nose, and hair roots as well as in my mouth. I would often go there on my own, not to buy, but just to browse. I was a bread-browser.

At the grocer's the piquant fragrance of fresh-ground coffee would make me shudder. I would turn my back toward people lest they see, perhaps laugh at, this poor boy's shameless indulgence in rich sensuality.

Garlic garlands hung from nails on the walls along with braided necklaces of violet onions and Oriental figs strung on hemp. The spigots of dark, soggy barrels dripped oil and vinegar, which was sold "loose." Beans, barley, sugar, peas, salt, rice, pepper, cloves, allspice, cinnamon sticks, thyme, poppy seeds lay exposed in open sacks. I walked around not only smelling them but visualizing the ports of call from which they had come, a multiple sense experience that today might be described as smellavision.

❀ ❀ ❀

Against the vibrant smells of edibles there was a running counterpoint of audibles, the voices of the people.

Mr. Man's shop was a stronghold of democracy, an open forum in which the mamas and the owner engaged in what today is called a dialogue. At that time it was more like a heated *ad hominem* debate in which claims were refuted, allegations hurled, exceptions taken, motives impugned. Those confrontations were my first lessons in ideological warfare.

"I don't like the looks of this codfish."

"Lady"—when he called her "lady" he no longer thought she was—"for looks you don't buy codfish; you buy goldfish."

"Mister, this chicken has a broken leg."

"Look, lady, you gonna eat it or dance with it?"

"Yesterday in the dozen eggs you sold me was two stinkin' eggs. Shall I bring them back?"

"No, lady. Your word is as good as the eggs."

"Listen, my friend the butcher, before you weigh the meat, take out the bones."

"I buy with bones; you'll buy with bones."

"I don't pay for no bones."

"Alright. No bones."

"Thank you. You're a gentleman. Now put the bones in a separate bag for soup. Thank you. Now, never mind the meat. I don't like your meat anyhow."

By her order the butcher could guess what was going on at the lady's home. If she went from chopped meat to lamb chops, it meant her daughter Rosie was finally bringing home a feller for dinner. "Very nice, very nice," said the butcher. When the lady went to steak, the butcher said, "Congratulations." He knew it meant that the feller was bringing the ring that night. And when the lady went back to chopped meat, he knew that the feller had married Rosie and moved in with the family. He said nothing.

Our mamas did not hesitate to bargain. Questioning a price was standard procedure.

"How much are these cucumbers?"

"Two for five."

The mama pushed one aside. "And how much is this one?"

"Three cents."

"Okay, I'll take the other one."

Fair trade meant that you never paid the asking price. All deals were negotiable, a custom that in America goes at least as far back as the purchase of Manhattan Island.

When one mama was caught shoplifting, the butcher naturally did not press charges. "Just pay for the chicken and we'll forget what happened."

Tears of gratitude running down her face, she kissed his, sobbing, "I don't know why I did it, and I swear to you I'll never do it again. I'll be glad to pay for it, but not at your prices, you crook, you!"

Making a good deal called for every known technique and stratagem of logic and pseudologic, deduction, induction, seduction, abduction, thesis, hypothesis, and antithesis. Rich people could afford logical reasoning: Parker sells good suits. This is a Parker suit. Therefore this is a good suit.

People like Mama, however, who could not risk spending an extra penny, questioned everything: Parker sells good suits? This is a good suit? Who said so—Parker?

When I was about to be graduated from elementary school, Mama took me to the pushcart market to buy me a tie. I was the last of her kids, and she was going to treat me to my first brand-new, never-handed-down tie.

The tie man asked fifty cents, and, to my utter astonishment, Mama paid it—no counteroffer, no debate, no dissent, just fifty cents paid politely in cash, without comment, and "Thank you" yet, to close the deal.

I didn't dare ask. As we walked home Mama read my mind. "Sammy, you are wondering why your mother paid the fifty cents without a word. Well, you are young yet. Some day you'll understand. I never liked that man. I'm getting even.

85

Tonight he will kill himself because he didn't ask me a dollar."

⚘ ⚘ ⚘

The candy-store man eked out a living mainly from kids. There is no harder way to eke it. When jelly beans were ten for a penny we would demand five whites, three greens, two yellows, "And you owe me one pink from last time, remember? You were all out of pinks, and you said 'I'll owe you a pink,' so today you owe me a pink, right? But I don't want no pinks because I don't like pinks, but my brother, he likes pinks, and he'll take away my pinks, so give me reds for pinks."

Two-for-a-penny items allowed for mixed deals. "Give me one of these and one of those." The only way the candy-store man could tell "these" from "those" was to stick his head and right arm into the showcase, pointing and calling out in muffled tones from under glass, "These?"

"No, those."

"Frying pans?"

"No. Over there near the lickwich shoelaces next to the sugar cushions. No, not those, those are foxy grandpas. Behind the pink bananas, right in front of the barber poles, over there near the root-beer barrels. No, not those, those are Mary Janes. Never mind, give me chocolate babies, all boys!" (There was a widely accepted belief that you got more chocolate that way.)

We formed partnerships for the purpose of mass purchasing. "You wanna go halfies on chicken feed? How about we go threezies on a ice cream cone? No free licks!" We might even go fourzies and fivezies on Abraham Lincoln lozenge pennies, and tenzies on long strips of paper with sugar dots glued on them.

In return for our patronage the candy-store man had to supply us kids with drinks of water in the summertime as a

86

public service. At the height of one August heat wave he put up a sign: *Penny candy free. Water one cent.*

Adults were too embarrassed to ask for a free glass of water. They bought seltzer, either plain or (more expensive) sweetened with cherry, pineapple, or strawberry syrup. The most popular flavor was cherry, with a real live cherry at the bottom of the glass, and sometimes a straw, but rarely a spoon. There was a diabolical scheme behind the cherry drink which brought customers back again and again. It capitalized on the thirst in man, not so much for seltzer or cherries but for the solution of a problem: How to get at the cherry, which had developed an attachment for the glass. Use the finger? Not nice in public. Lifting it up with two straws might have worked in Chinatown, but this was not Chinatown and there was only one straw.

I watched normally dignified men standing in front of the soda counter pounding the deseltzered glass into their faces, first gently, then violently, trying in vain to dislodge the cherry, which seemed glued to the bottom. Some men, the weaker ones, gave up in disgust, others stayed on for as long as fifteen minutes tilting, tapping, blowing, and sucking.

Some mamas kept a seltzer man on a retainer. He would come to the house once a week to leave an order of heavy blue siphon bottles, which served as stomach fire extinguishers. The concentration of carbonization in those bottles was enough to revive the dead. "You don't have a bottle of seltzer in the house? What do you do if, God forbid, somebody faints?"

The drugstore on our block, or anywhere else, was easily identifiable. The window display was standard: two large apothecary jars filled with a red or blue liquid, a mortar and pestle, a plaster cast of fallen arches, several little dishes of medicinal herbs, a sexually neuter dummy wearing trusses above and below the belt, a model of an open chest showing the human lungs and heart, and a live cat dozing in the corner.

The older folks called him the "druggisman"; the younger ones called him "Doc." He wore a striped shirt, no jacket, and a professional expression. No one would deal with anyone in the shop but Doc. "This other guy [his apprentice] could give me the wrong physic and kill me."

If you gave him a prescription, he hummed as he studied it, and guessed at what your trouble was. If he couldn't guess, you really had something to worry about.

"Tell me the truth, Doc. What have I got?"

"I'm not sure, but let me know if this stuff is any good. I think I've got it myself."

Doc provided a variety of essential services, only a small part of which were pharmaceutical. His shop was a first-aid station for street accidents. Removing foreign bodies from kids' bodies kept him busy all day long. It was he, too, who provided some elementary "personal" education for growing girls and for mothers who had stopped growing.

❁ ❁ ❁

There were itinerant vendors of goods and services, always the same men, who came into our street but rarely into our homes. They announced their arrival by familiar street calls or other attention-getting devices.

The rag man carried a rolled-up newspaper in his hand and sang out, "I cash clothes." The burlap bag he carried over his shoulder gave rise to a story (probably apocryphal) that became part of the local folklore: A woman waved to him to come up to the fifth floor, then asked him into her apartment. "I hate to bother you, but do me a favor. Tell my rotten kid that if he doesn't finish his cereal you'll take him away in your bag."

The ices man scraped the surface off a cake of ice with a metal scoop, then poured flavored syrup from hair-tonic bottles onto the mound of shavings to create dirty sherbets we called "snowballs."

The lemonade man pushed a cart on which there was an inverted ten-gallon glass jug containing fresh-drowned insects floating about in yellowish embalming fluid.

The frankfurter man came with his umbrella'd rickshaw carrying a tank full of split-skinned hot dogs that protruded beyond their rolls. Tasting the dripping mustard without immediately digging your teeth into the soft flesh of the frankfurter called for some first-class self-control. (Our ice cream cone training helped.) The sweet-potato man, the pretzel man, the coconut man, the watermelon man, and the peanut man would race to get to us ahead of the frankfurter man.

There were music men too. A German oom-pah-pah band played in front of our tenement each morning. If you sucked a lemon in front of them (and we did), their mouths would pucker and they couldn't oom or pah.

Long-haired violinists gave short recitals in the backyards. Soft-hearted mamas would wrap a penny in a piece of newspaper and throw it out to them. The artist would stop his performance in the middle of a bar of "East Side, West Side," put the penny in his pocket, remove his hat, bow to his patroness with an exquisite flourish like a bullfighter, then continue. Two pennies or more got an encore of the "Toreador Song" from *Carmen*.

An old lady came by every day pushing an even older baby carriage on the seat of which was a tray of strange notions intended not for us kids but for our mothers—spools of thread, scissors, clothespins, matches, combs, elastic, teething rings, religious items, bobbins, and tonics. She had no name because she had no specific merchandise. She wasn't a man, and you couldn't call her "our lady of the bobbins," but the women always "took from her" because she was a widow, "even if she costs a penny more." A widow lady, Mama used to say, "comes even ahead of a grocery man."

VIII

Mama, It's Cold Inside

❀ ❀ ❀

Mr. Man is gone, and I am the poorer for it. We were personally involved in each other's daily lives. Part of me died when progress declared him expendable. A world that can pronounce him dead in the interest of efficiency can do the same to me. If there were a few words of post-mortem praise spoken at his graveside, they were drowned out by the fanfare for the new supermarket that replaced him. Man is dead. Long live Management.

The grand opening of a supermarket is marked by the kind of pageantry that in other epochs marked the coronation of an emperor, the beatification of a saint, the lifting of a thirty-year siege, the birth of a male heir to the throne, or the winning of national independence. Emissaries of government, commerce, and church come to read proclamations, cut ribbons, bless parking lots, and pledge allegiance to the flags of the Monarchy of Merchandising.

I do not believe that "super" equals "superior" or that man

became superman in the supermarket. To my eyes he got smaller and smaller until he disappeared into no-man's-land.

Mr. Man is no longer in the doorway to greet me with a "Good morning, how are you, how's the family?" He has been supplanted by a beam of spooky blue light (the evil eye?), which I cross, triggering a cheery musical ping in C major, the electronic substitute for "Good morning, how are you, how's the family?" The IN door then swings open. Once the door has pinged, you cannot unping yourself. If you want OUT, you must proceed ahead, turn left, and leave through the pong door. A deliberate or accidental passing through a door marked NI or TUO sets off an alarm in Security indicating a customer escape. I still like doors I can push open with the palm of my hand. I don't mind the warmth left over from other people's hands.

The supermarket is too much for me. I am easily overwhelmed by overabundance, by "full" dribbling over into "fulsome." Even the superlative may be superfluous. While the supermarkets fills my needs, it also whets my greeds. The glut of goods breeds gluttony. Enough is heavenly; too much is hell, the hell of indecision.

We have come a long way from the outhouse when bathroom tissue is offered in enough varieties to reflect the décor and/or the accessories of that special place and/or the personality of the person or persons making personal use thereof. Yellow? Blue? Chartreuse? Plaid? Perfumed? Rose? Gardenia? Soft? Facial? Squeezable? Single-strength? Double-strength? Heavy-duty . . . ?

I have seen many an opulence-stricken mother standing in front of a loaded display case from which she must select one, just one, container of cottage cheese. In Mama's time cottage cheese was just cottage cheese, and it came in only two brands —fresh or let-him-feed-it-to-*his*-children! For the modern young mother, consumer paralysis sets in quickly as she struggles to choose from among creamed cottage cheese; uncreamed, skimmed, partly skimmed, and unskimmed cottage cheese; salt-free and cream-free; bungalow style, California style, and popcorn style; small-curd and large-curd; improved (it now contains "ingredients"), new improved, new new improved . . .

At the end of her sleeve is her kid tugging away. "Ma! I'm hungry, Ma."

"Wait a minute! Can't you see I'm trying to decide?"

Outside, the husband is going round and round the market, honking his horn as he passes the entrance, yelling "Come on already!"

"Wait a minute! I'm deciding . . ."

To us bread was just bread. We just asked God to give us our daily bread. And God knew and we knew what we were talking about. Bread! Amen!

Today's woman must choose from among breads that are nonfattening, unfattening, or defattening; enriched, nonenriched, or re-enriched; thin-sliced, thick-sliced, round-sliced or unsliced; slo-baked, fast-baked, baked-while-you-sleep; with or without seeds; with or without raisins; with or without vitamin B added; Jewish, Italian, or French daily breads with or without Amen.

"Ma! I'm hungry, Ma!"

Honk! Honk!

"Come on already!"

We used to describe a person in trouble as being "in a pickle." The woman in front of this pickle shelf is in a superpickle. Dill? Half-dill? Sour? Half-sour? Sliced? Unsliced? Vertically sliced? Horizontally sliced? In mustard sauce, in brine, in a jar, a bottle, a glass, soft or hard plastic containers . . . ?

"Stop chewing on my sleeve!"

"I'm hungry!"

"Suck your thumb!"

Honk! Honk!

"Come on already!"

"Just let me pick up some ice cream for dessert."

Vanilla? Cherry vanilla? Vanilla cherry? Chocolate crunched marbled vanilla? Vanilla smashed marbled chocolate? Italian crumbled marble tutti frutti? Rum strawberry banana chipped pineapple? Popsicles, conesicles, sticksicles, tartsicles; icicles, double popsicles, double conesicles, double sticksicles . . . ?

Honk! Honk!

"Come on already."

"Let's get out of here. We're going to eat out!"

To compound the confusion, Mama's chicken has been dismembered. It has been neatly disjointed and all its organs sorted out and filed into plastic see-through bags. The young housewife has been spared the bloody ordeal of chicken surgery. Chicken can now be bought in parts. Anyone can create his own version of a chicken out of a do-it-yourself chicken kit. Put together two heads, one eye, three breasts, four feet, add a mandolin, and you've got yourself an original poultry Picasso.

The supermarket herring, too, is worth studying as an example of the disintegration of classical unities, the division and subdivision of natural entities into unnatural segments and fractions of segments. The complete herring (head, eye, body, tail) is rapidly becoming an aquarium exhibit. We can now lay hands on only part of a herring, or part of a part of a herring. Heads and tails have been discarded as unsightly throwbacks to some barbaric era when our ancestors sucked fish bones. (Some living relatives still do, but they don't get invited very often.)

Mama bought a total herring. She used to go to the corner herring man, station herself in front of a barrel packed tightly with hundreds of herrings, and go into a trance. She was getting a message from a herring. "The one on the bottom." (No good herring could ever be found near the top.)

"Toward the right or the left?" the herring man would ask.

"The right."

He would roll his sleeve up to his shoulder, plunge his arm so far down that his head was resting on herrings, and come up with a herring. Her eyes still closed, Mama would say, "That's not the one!" He would have to make several more dives before coming up with *the* one. (To me all herrings looked alike, but not to an authority like Mama.) She would not snap out of her trance until the herring she had contacted had been fished out.

At home Mama would cut the herring into as many slices as there were eaters, plus two for expected unexpected guests, slip a little onion under its head, and leave it there to wait for dinner.

On more than one occasion my brothers sent me to steal a slice of herring, a procedure that is utterly different from, let's say, stealing a pencil or an apple. You pulled out the slice from the middle, then carefully moved both ends in, making a shorter herring and leaving no traces of a robbery. By the time my father got to bless the herring, there was nothing left to bless but an eye and a tail—and Mama stood there swearing to God she had bought a whole herring.

Getting out of the supermarket is much more difficult than getting in. It is somewhat like leaving a foreign country. "What do you have to declare?" The check-out counter looks and operates like the U.S. Customs. There are two lanes marked *Local,* two *Express,* one *Ten items or less,* and seven lanes marked *This lane closed.* Any lane may be closed at the discretion of the customs officer if said lane should become dangerously overcrowded by one person.

The cashier checks your bags for undeclared or contraband goods.

"Where did you get this ketchup?"

"From the shelf marked 'ketchup.' "

"This is not our ketchup."

"I'm sorry. It must have been in the bag when I started from home."

The cashier shoves it aside and stamps it "Confiscated."

Our old grocery man never could have gotten away with making his customers stand in line. They had their own honor system known as "next."

"Who's next?"

"I'm next."

"I have the next next after her next."

"I'm sorry, my next is before your next."

"I would give you my next, but I already gave it to somebody else."

"Look, we don't have to fight. You can have my next."

"Okay. But next time watch your own next."

"Can I have your next? I got a husband at home."

"We all got troubles."

In order to avoid conflicts in pecking order at the supermarket delicatessen counter the customer pulls a numbered ticket from a machine and then waits to be called. (Even shoplifters must take a number.)

"Who's got 8?"

(Silence)

"Somebody's gotta have 8."

(Silence)

"Will 8 please come forward and be recognized?"

(Silence)

Voice in crowd: "There ain't no 8."

"There's gotta be a 8!"

"Who's got 8? My milk is turning sour."

"Somebody took his 8 and left!"

"Okay. So who's got 9?"

"I got 9."

"Blue or yellow?"

"Blue."

"That's yesterday's 9. Come back tomorrow."

Mama's grocery man added up the bill right on the brown-paper bag with a heavy black pencil-crayon that he carried over his ear. The lady then checked his addition, item for item.

"What's this nine cents?"

"I'm sorry, it's a mistake. It's supposed to be a seven."

"So make another mistake and make it a six."

The supermarket cashier clicks off each item on a register. Gears hum, numbers fly, and $21.40 (no matter what you buy) appears on a ticker tape. It comes to about $5.00 per inch of tape.

Before milady can even think, What's this nine cents? she is handed several strips of trading stamps. This act of super-generosity leaves her limp with gratitude. The shopping bag now looks like an anonymously donated Thanksgiving basket. As she leaves, loaded down with goodies, she counts her stamps instead of her change.

Many people are buying things they don't need to get the stamps they do need so they can trade them in for things they don't need.

"How many stamps do I get for a loaf of bread?"

"Three stamps."

"Give me thirty breads so I can get a Weight Watcher's Calorie Counter."

"How many stamps is a round trip to Bermuda?"

"Two hundred thousand."

"How many bars of soap do I have to buy?"

"Seven hundred thousand."

"How many for one way?"

Once she gets home she takes stock. "Let's see if I have

everything. I got my stamps, my stamp catalogue, the stamp contest forms, this week's *Stamp News* . . . Now, what did I forget? My God! I forgot Georgie!

"Hello, is this the supermarket? If you have a kid named Georgie around there, send him home."

"Sorry, we don't deliver."

One of the newer forms of togetherness is spending an evening at home with the family, licking stamps.

"Ma, I got homework to do."

"Shut up and keep licking! We're almost up to a set of encyclopedias."

Some schoolteachers have raised individual grades considerably by offering stamps for every test mark over 85 instead of the old-fashioned gold star.

Anyone who wanted to wipe out this nation would only have to poison the glue on our trading stamps.

One day I heard the voice of Mama's man on the check-out line. He seemed to have come back from the dead to speak up not for himself alone but for all the meek who have inherited efficiency but lost their democratic right to talk, question, complain, haggle, dissent, or to say and to hear a "How are you today?" (A marquee that says: *Special today fresh-killed chicken* is not quite the same as "Psst, Mrs. Levenson. Have I got a chicken for you! You'll lick your fingers from it.")

Mr. P., the hero of the check-out line, had once been a grocery man himself, but was forced out of business by the supermarkets. He now bought his own groceries at the big store. Once he was about halfway home when he realized he had been given the wrong change. He rushed back, went to the end of the line, waited his turn, and finally got his chance.

"I'm sorry, but you gave me the wrong change."

"When did this happen?"

"I'd say about twenty minutes ago."

The check-out man rose to his full national-chain width and height, pointed imperiously to a sign on the wall, and asked, "Do you see what that sign says?"

"I don't see so good no more. What does it say?"

"It says: 'All errors in change must be reported at time of check-out or they will not be rectified. Signed: The Management.'"

"You mean it's too late?"

"I'm afraid so."

"All right," Mr. P. said as he walked out. "Too late is too late. I just wanted you to know you gave me three dollars too much."

IX

There's No Present Like the Time

I have felt the time of my life ebbing away as I marked time not only in supermarkets but in front or back, inside or outside of airports, service stations, buses, elevators, restaurants, banks, post offices, box offices, doctors' and dentists' offices, information desks, reservation desks, confirmation desks. It's all the more frustrating because I had rushed to get there to save time, and because it is happening to me *now* at the height of the instamatic age. I don't want speed; I want time. I would like to take my time, but it is being taken from me. Help! I'm being robbed!

Mama lived *with* time, but not *on* time or *for* time. She measured time not by seconds, minutes, or hours, but by the milestones and tombstones that marked the road of her life. "May God give us time; troubles will come by themselves." *What time* it happened seemed trivial to Mama as against what happened *at the time*. *When* seemed much less important than *to whom* and *how* she felt when "it" happened.

99

Her moments of truth were imprinted on the heart rather than on the calendar. They were not just happenings, but happinessings and unhappinessings, full of emotional as well as historical impact—holidays, disasters, births, deaths, miracles, narrow escapes, handed down, as the Bible was, by word of mouth.

"When was I born, Mama?"

"How could I forget? You were born on the night the Titanic sank."

When the time came to register us at school, the clerk demanded more exact dates of birth. She refused to write down Mama's "It was on the third day of Passover."

The clerk tried to nail Mama down.

"Ask your mother when you moved to your present address."

"Ma, when did we move to where we live now?"

"Right after Bill got the croup, after Mike got the whooping cough, right after Albert's mumps on both cheeks, nobody should know from such trouble."

"Ma, when did you become a citizen."

"How could I forget? It was on the day of Aunt Annie's wedding. How do I remember it so good? Because I wasn't invited, that's how!"

"Ma, how old was Grandpa when he died?"

"Well, if he had lived till next week he would be dead forty years."

Time had purpose, and not always a purpose of one's choice. Mama had prepared us. There is a time, she said time and again, for weeping and a time for rejoicing, and for lighting memorial candles, a time for silence, for speaking, a time to come home and a time to leave home, a time for dying (and she would spit three times, poo, poo, poo), and "time a big boy like you should know better than to say 'Tomorrow I will go . . .' Only a fool says 'Tomorrow we will.' If God will live and be healthy, and Papa will be all right too, then we'll see." To avoid disappointments you didn't make appointments. "If you're there before it's over, you're on time."

She defied the tyranny of clock time. Exact time was too exacting. She could do little about the space she lived in, but she could handle time. "You have to stay up all night to study? What's your hurry? So you'll graduate a week later." All in good time. When the radio announcer said, "At the sound of the chime it will be exactly two o'clock," she turned to the set and said, "And if it's two minutes after two, so you'll get arrested?"

"This minute, this minute," she would mumble. "Everybody's gotta know about this minute. Tell me better where did the years go?"

Daylight Saving Time, she said, is like cutting off the end of a blanket and sewing it on to the other end to make it longer. After the summer you cut it off again and put it back where you cut it off to make it shorter. "Very smart."

All this playing around with our timetable may have thrown us out of sync with eternity, and the millennium may never come.

Mama did not live in our clock-eyed world. She could tell the passing of time in each day without looking at the clock. Our flat was a sunless dial. When the light of dawn arrived at her bedroom window (always a little late, since it had to climb over tall tenements to get there), it was time for waking and working. Light coming through the kitchen window meant that her children would soon be home from school for lunch. By early afternoon (darkness came early for us) the rays of the setting sun would briefly touch our front-room windows, signaling to Mama that the day was over and the time for the labors of night had arrived. Yet for at least a half hour she defiantly would not turn on the lights. "I got time."

She certainly couldn't count on our family's collection of timeworn timepieces. Some had faces and no hands; others had time on their hands and no faces. Our eight-day alarm clock ran for about an hour, but took about eight days to wind. Every one of my brothers still has a dent on his thumb from winding it. It went only if you laid it face down, so it could keep the hour a secret from Mama. Twice a day it would go into convulsions—tremble, wheeze, and scare the daylights into anyone still sleeping.

Mama believed that for anything (or for anybody) to come out right, time was the indispensable ingredient. She cooked a chicken for a minimum of six hours (always on a low flame —what was the hurry?), dropping in an onion at the proper moment, tasting its effect at another proper moment, wiggling the pot, blowing on a spoonful of the broth and then sipping it with closed eyes, shaking her head in doubt or nodding approval.

Sometimes she left me in charge. "I'm going next door for a minute; stir the soup every half hour." I sat there listening to the cover chitti-chattering jazzily on the hot pot like a drummer's cymbal, chicken-cha, chicken-cha, chickety chickety chicketty cha. I joined in, beating a spoon on the side of the pot, chicken cha boom boom, chicken cha boom, chicketty cha, completely carried away with the rhythm while the soup boiled over, adding sizzly shi sha to chicken-ch-boom boom. Only when Mama timpanized me on the head with the wet ladle did I come out of my fantasy.

When a cake was in the oven an aura of mystery fell over the house. The shades were drawn, windows shut, neighbors informed. Mama moved cautiously about in house slippers. She knew nothing about thermodynamics. She knew only that a sponge cake is supposed to rise slowly and that the slightest sneeze within an area of twenty miles could cause a collapse.

Happy Sammy would come home from school, slam the door, and hear a horrible scream from the kitchen: "Murderer! You killed my cake!"

To confirm her fears, he would open the oven door a crack to take a peek, let in the cold air, and kill the cake.

She would then chase me through the house brandishing a dough-mixing spoon at me, scattering wet confetti through the air, yelling, "I'll flatten you out like you flattened my cake!"

I would rush out of the house, slamming the door behind me for the second time, this time so violently that the building came near to collapsing with the cake. As I ran down the street I could see Mama at the closed window shaking her fist and hear her yelling, "Cake-killer!"

❀ ❀ ❀

Mama's food not only took time but also left you with something to remember for a long time afterward. She guaranteed it would "melt in your mouth." It did. It was not supposed to harden again in the stomach, but it did. A light, fluffy matzoh ball could dissolve under your tongue and reconstitute itself into a billiard ball; a delicate potato pancake could be reborn as a hockey puck.

In addition to time, Mama had instinct on her side. My sister Dora tried in vain to fathom the mystique of instinct baking.

"How much flour do you use, Ma?"

"What do you mean, how much do I use?"

"I mean a cup, a half cup . . . ?"

"What do you need cups for? You use your head."

"Okay. So how many eggs?"

"Not too many."

"How much sugar?"

"Not too much."

"How much salt?"

"Not too salty."

"How much water?"

"A mouthful."

"What! Okay. So how long do I leave it in the oven?"

"It shouldn't burn."

To find out whether a cake was ready Mama would pull a straw out of a broom, stick it into the hot dough, then study it like a thermometer. We never understood just what signs she was looking for; we knew only that at our house we had lots of burned cakes and bald brooms.

Dora, surprisingly, learned to comprehend and even to use incomprehensible recipes like: "When huckleberries are expensive, prunes make better grape jelly than raspberries."

X

Panic Button

It took us fifteen years of postmarital saving to earn our own home, a lovely place, equipped with all the latest conveniences. "How did people live a hundred years ago without all these electronic devices?" we asked ourselves. The answer, of course, was obvious. They had all died.

Some day our grandchildren are going to ask about us, "How did they live *with* all those conveniences?" I can tell them right now. "Kids, it wasn't easy!" We had been trained by our parents only for living with people, since people were about the only possessions we had. We had to retrain ourselves for living with people-free paraphernalia.

I am not ungrateful for what the machine has done for me. I, me, Sam, formerly Sammy, the kid from the dark tenements who sought the sunlight, can now create his own light, day or night, by pushing a button. Let there be light! Let there be heat, cold, sound, music, pictures. I have been granted the power of On and Off; Onipotence and Offipotence.

I am also not ungrateful for America's practical idealism, for its noble concern with emancipating us from manual slavery by creating machines to take over the drudgerous jobs.

Somehow this ideal (as has happened to a lot of other lofty ideals) has run into trouble. We, the people, are now working for the machines that are supposed to be working for us. The hours may be better, but we don't seem very happy with the new boss.

We have created machines in our own image. They are so human that they behave like human beings—mean, irritable, lazy, stubborn, spiteful, wasteful, even neurotic and psychotic. They, too, can lose their buttons. They don't get along with each other or with us. They blame their breakdowns on us; we blame ours on them. They resent, above all, our pretensions to immortality. We have a hereafter, we tell them—you don't. They get angry and retaliate: "We'll show you who's going to outlast whom! Let's see who breaks down first. Ready! Go!"

❀ ❀ ❀

My machines sportingly grant me a head start, confident that they will beat me in the end. Either I get up a half hour early in the morning to start plugging in or I stay up a half hour later to turn the dial that sets the clock that starts the coffee that triggers the thermostat that flips the switch that starts the oil burner that blows the fuse that shuts off the alarm and everything else that lives in the house that Sam built. We eat by candlelight quite often. It's so romantic.

Our dream house is large enough to accommodate a goodly number of nightmares. The air-conditioner and the oil burner have a little game of their own, just for laughs—and I think I know whom they're laughing at. When the air-conditioner brings the room temperature down to 68 degrees the oil burner sends up the heat. When the room temperature goes up to 72 degrees the air-conditioner starts again.

Our electric coffee grinder sometimes doesn't grind, but the air-conditioner always does. Our ice-cube maker sometimes doesn't make ice, but our air-conditioner always does. It also has a something called a "directional," which guarantees that no matter where I sleep, it will find me and direct a stream of icy air onto the back of my neck. It can even follow me into the next room. We now have more colds in the summer than in the winter, even though we use an electric blanket from May to September, not without considerable marital discord over who shall have custody of the controls. My wife likes her feet well done; I like mine medium. Fall asleep at the switch and you can be quietly fried to death.

Our toaster works on either AC or DC, but not on bread. It has two settings—too soon and too late. *I* like my toast dark. *It* likes it light. If I try to hold the toast down to get it darker, I can feel the toaster fighting back. If I take my hand off the lever, it will either hurl the toast angrily into the air or hold it down until it becomes a square of charcoal. "Okay, Sam. You wanted dark? You've got it dark."

Our electric can opener cuts through any straight line but cannot negotiate the curves. It stops and waits for us to move it ahead to the next straight line. We end up with a can opened on all four sides but attached at the four corners. We have to cut them with a hand can opener, which not only opens cans but hands.

Our washing machine, no sooner had we bought it, developed a serious character defect. It steals socks. There was nothing I could do about it, since the guarantee does not cover moral imperfections.

The dishwasher is no problem at all. First you scrape off the food, sponge the dishes in the sink in hot soapy water (the machine doesn't like dirty dishes), rinse, stack the nice clean dishes in the nice clean machine, and turn the knob. After about ten minutes you remove the dishes, wash off the soap stains, dry the dishes with a towel, and put them back in the dish closet.

Since we are a small family, my thrifty wife will not turn the machine on until a good-size dishload has accumulated. "It doesn't pay to use up so much electricity for so few dishes." We have considered getting two sets of dishes, one for eating and washing, and another for the dishwasher.

Our kitchen sink has a disposal unit that has a built-in man-made monster with ferocious built-in teeth with which it grinds up bones. If you don't feed it bones it becomes tame and cannot handle anything heavier than Pablum. My wife began to ask around for bones. This started a neighborhood rumor that we were on the rocks. We began to eat out so that we could bring home doggie bags. That scheme came to an abrupt finish when one waiter asked our daughter Emily, "What's your doggie's name?" and she said, "Westinghouse."

Our wall oven protects us against Mama's hit-or-miss timing with a sophisticated meter that is supposed to shut off the oven when the meat is ready. It also has a little window through which we can watch fifteen dollars' worth of meat being cremated.

Those who do not have electronic oven timers can use thermometers that are inserted into the meat. Medical bulletins are then issued: "Condition satisfactory," "As well as can be expected," "Critical," and "Call the nearest of kin to dinner."

Our kitchen has hoods, fans, vents, and exhausts that keep the air clean while we are out in the backyard broiling over coals that smoke into our faces. Any smoke we have not sucked into our lungs works its way back to the kitchen, where the hoods, fans, vents, and exhausts filter it out, shooting fresh smoke back into the yard for us to breathe in.

Many an afternoon as we sat in the backyard listening to the birds coughing we have mused about the progress we have made. In our tenement days we ate inside the house, and if you had to go to the (as Mama would have said, "You should excuse the expression") toilet, you went outside. Now we eat outside, and if you have to "go," you go inside.

Science has made all this progress possible, but it has also had to train doctors to treat the accidental side effects of the instant-electronic-automated good life, such as barbecued eyeballs (from peering into the toaster to see why it doesn't pop); the AC-DC shakes (from the constant use of electric toothbrushes, razors, shoe buffers, and scalp massagers); indoor snow blindness (from searching for a hamburger lost in the back of a freezer); karate wrist (from banging the hand violently against a nonoperating coin-operated vending machine).

I once had quite a run-in with a vending machine.

My wife had asked me to pick up a container of milk. It was Sunday. The stores were closed. I pulled my car up to a milk-vending machine. Calmly I proceeded to read the instructions on the machine. I didn't go to college for nothing.

Insert coins here.

I inserted coins here. Nothing happened.

Pick up merchandise below.

There was no merchandise below.

I pushed the lever marked *Coin return*. No coins were returned.

I felt like an idiot and looked like one in the mirror on the machine. Look, Sam, look. See the shnook?

I found a sticker on the side that read: "If out of order, call 684-279-4462 Ext. 7218." I put a dime into the nearest phone and I called 684-279-4462 Ext. 7218.

"We are sorry. This is a live operator. Our recorded tape is temporarily out of order. The number you are calling is temporarily out of order"—and my dime disappeared, permanently.

I said "Thank you" (Mama's training) and went back to

the milk machine. It now looked like a Las Vegas gambling machine, and I was hooked. I'm gonna go for broke. I put in more coins. This time I heard some groaning. No milk. No money. Just a sign that lit up: *Make your next selection.* I selected to kick the machine. Still no milk. Just some cold hot chocolate in my shoes.

Ashamed to come home empty-handed, I tried to call my wife. My dime fell in, but the call did not go through. To get a dime back from the phone company takes two dimes. The first for losing, and the second for telling the operator you lost the first dime, which the operator tells you will be returned in five two-cent postage stamps or in the form of a ten-cent check, which costs the company eight cents to mail. (The reverse, getting your dime back by accident, is one of the greatest joys known to man, topped only by being able to say to an operator, "Yes, you did return my dime by mistake, but I cannot redeposit it. If you will send me *your* name and address . . .") I gave the operator all the vital statistics necessary to reclaim my first dime, then attempted to call home on the second dime. This dime fell on the floor of the phone booth.

You can't bend over in a phone booth. I tried and banged my head. I opened the door and stepped out of the booth so I could see the dime, but the light went out inside the booth. Now I couldn't see the dime. I closed the door from the outside, so the light went on. I could now see the dime, but the door was closed. So I opened the door to reach the dime. The light went out. Now I couldn't see the dime. I stretched out on the sidewalk outside the booth and opened the door halfway, just enough to keep the light on, and I began to feel around inside the booth. That was when the lady stepped on my hand, and we each let out a howl. A kind policeman took me home, sans milk, sans money, sans mind.

If I had to, I could also learn to live without Minute Car Laundries whose giant brushes make old scratches look like new, bring out the rust spots, and remove the registration stickers. Whatever the machines have forgotten, "the boys" will finish. *Don't forget the boys* says the sign. It's hard to forget them with your feet in four inches of water, your pants glued to a wet seat, your inside mirror facing out, your outside mirror facing in, your safety belt jammed under your seat, your antenna gone, and your floor mats missing as you drive off into the rain.

My mother could have gotten along fine without the invention of the wheel. With eight kids and Papa to look after, she couldn't go anywhere anyhow. My wife has two children and lots of places to go, and she has the wheels to get her there, but she can't leave the house, because a man is coming to do for her the one thing she can no longer do for herself —repair the machines that are supposed to do everything for her.

Our doorbell went out of order. It is no ordinary doorbell. You push an illuminated pearl button on the outside, which sets off a four-minute concerto for glockenspiel and chimes inside. The doorbell in Mama's house was not truly a bell but a box that contained the remnants of a bell. Its button had disappeared into the woodwork, leaving a small circular opening into which you inserted the tip of your pinky, making contact with shreds of copper wire, which apparently drew enough electricity from your body to relay a message to a small box over the molding in the kitchen. It had been painted over so many times that it had lost all of its ding and most of its ling. We had an auxiliary system of communication between visitors and our family which Mama called the "Whozit." Downstairs, over the letter boxes, was a mouthpiece into which the caller yelled "Hello" and Mama yelled back into her mouthpiece "Whozit?"

When the fancy doorbell at our home canceled all its concerts without notice, my wife called the electrician. She waited four days for him to show up. On the fifth day she apologetically called him on the phone again. "I was there yesterday," he swore. "I rang the doorbell, but nobody answered. Besides, I can't come today. I can't leave my place. I'm waiting for my plumber."

When we moved into the house we received a blender in the mail by mistake. Without opening the box, we mailed it back to the company. In two weeks it was back again with a note: "We have repaired your blender." There was a small charge for $7.80 for parts, and a postage charge of $1.25. We did not pay. We stuck the thing in the back of a closet, sealed up in its box, and neither the blender nor the company has given us any more trouble.

❁ ❁ ❁

Among the old-timers there are pockets of resistance still being held by indomitable anti-automation guerrilla fighters, brave last-ditch partisans of the old methods who will never surrender. The astronauts may go flying around in space at twenty-five thousand miles an hour, but these earth people are still spitting on pressing irons to find out if they are hot, measuring a yard from the tip of the nose to the tip of the outstretched hand, spraying laundry by mouth before ironing, and singing one chorus of "Sweet Rosie O'Grady" to time a three-minute egg.

I only recently saw a great Italian chef at work, a woman famous for her *al dente* spaghetti. She brought the water to a boil, dropped in the spaghetti, waited for a few minutes in front of the pot, then with the tip of a fork speared one hot strand for the test. She did not taste, pull, or squeeze it. She threw it against the white enamel door of her refrigerator and watched it slither down. By the rate of its descent she could tell whether or not it was *al dente*.

My mother-in-law not only clung to the old ways but poo-

poo'd every new device. Like so many of her contemporaries, she would not relinquish her old icebox. It stood in the same spot in the same kitchen for a generation. Hidden underneath it was the traditional pan, which had to be emptied regularly. Often there were hysterical screams in the night: "The pan!" She had even trained her children to be pan-handlers. "Two hands, not one hand; take short steps; don't make waves; don't laugh; don't cough; don't sneeze; wear shoes."

This woman was not ready for the second coming of the Ice Age. The entire concept of frozen foods gave her the chills.

Having tried in vain to persuade her mother to give up the old icebox in favor of a modern electric refrigerator, my wife went out and bought one. The delivery man was told to remove the old one.

When we went there for our customary Friday-night dinner we found the old icebox, pan and all, standing proudly side by side with its twentieth-century counterpart.

"You mean you're going to keep them both, Mama? Why do you need two iceboxes?"

"You know what I do?" she said. "I put a cake of ice in my old one, and the new one, I open the door wide, and it cools me off the whole house. By the way," she continued, "remember the electric broiler you sent me? That I can use! When I get up in the morning I turn the 'On' knob till it says 'No.' That starts the heat. Then I sit in front of it and let it bake my bad shoulder. Better than a doctor!"

There was a time when hunger was associated only with poverty. This is no longer true. I have seen wealthy families sitting around in luxurious homes pale and hungry, waiting for the dinner to thaw. (Very often a defrosted lamb chop may turn out to be a banana fritter.)

A husband coming home early may provoke a heated argument. "Never mind what you want to eat tonight. You can't walk in on me just like that and expect dinner just like that. Tell me what you want to eat next Tuesday; I have to start defrosting now."

One evening I found Conrad limping.

"What happened?"

"The ice cream fell on my foot."

My brother Joe tells me that when an ice pack is not available he instructs his patients to put a frozen chicken on the ailing spot.

A friend of ours has been deceiving her husband for years. He demands fresh, hand-squeezed orange juice for breakfast; she doesn't want to bother.

"The frozen stuff is just as good," says she.

"Nobody can fool me," says he. He looks for the pits. "Pits means fresh; no pits means frozen."

So she stores some pits in a teacup, drops them into his juice, waits for him to drink it and say "That's it; nobody can fool me," then puts the pits back into the teacup, ready for the next round trip.

❀ ❀ ❀

While the care and feeding of our conveniences has kept us parents busy, it has left our children without any important household chores other than eating and sleeping. They are our house guests, a status that gives them the leisure to sit around and listen with disbelief to my stories about Mama's magic-eye household appliances—the eight of us. We required no electricity. Mama just had to take one look at us with her magic eye and we started to work.

Since there was such a shortage of women in the brood, we were expected to do "woman's work." Mama said it would make us good husbands some day.

"Sweep under the beds!"

So we swept everything under the beds.

"Sweep under the carpet!"

We did. Everything we could find. Things reached the point where to get from the bedroom to the bathroom you had to go uphill.

Garbage disposal was easy. We used the fresh-air method. "You going for a walk? Take the garbage." It was not unusual to find yourself in the movies with a bag under your arm. It was also not unusual to take the wrong paper bag to work and find yourself with a strange lunch.

I cannot expect my children to do certain chores that have become extinct, like polishing the coal stove, bringing up the coal, changing the feathers from one pillow to another, oiling the clock, or fixing the toilet chain.

There is a good possibility that through a process of evolution tomorrow's children will be born adapted to the survival requirements of the new life. They will have one eight-fingered hand for pushing buttons, and a second hand, with only two fingers, located somewhere near the head, for purposes of scratching it. There will not be much else to do. The generation after that, children will say, "It's not automatic; you have to push a button."

There is something deep within me that resists and resents the chore of filling out bureaucratic questionnaires with crosses, checks, and circles, especially when I think of all the years I labored and of all the conscientious teachers who labored with me to improve my penmanship via the Palmer Method, a system of cultivating beautiful circles and oblique strokes guaranteed to give my handwriting the elegance of a papal secretary's. I remember the hours I was kept after school to get the curse out of my cursive writing. As the sun went down I sat there rounding and slanting on pages of lined yellow paper to the rhythm of the teacher's singsong:

"Round, round, and round we go, elbow off the ta-able! Wrist off the ta-ble! Up and down! Push, pull! Round-er! Round-er!" And I cannot forget the vows I made to my teachers never to forget correct spelling, grammar, syntax, syllabication, punctuation, and capitalization, and never to end my sentences with prepositions, and keep my participles from dangling, all "so that some day you may be able to express your thoughts more fully, Samuel."

Those rectangular boxes into which I must now fit the body of my thoughts look to me like small white coffins bordered in black. Don't box me in. Not yet. I'm still alive. . . .

They have spaces that need to be filled. *I* have needs that must be filled. I need to tell the whole story, not just the little part that fits the little hole. A mind repeatedly forced into blanks may finally become one. I am afraid I may suffer the fate of the supermarket chicken. Chicken in parts; Sam in parts. I, like the chicken, may end up with two heads, four legs, three eyes. "That's Sam?" Chopped Sam, maybe; whole Sam, never. When the parts of Sam become greater than the whole of Sam I'm ready for the last groundup.

I herewith inform the form-makers that I will not co-operate with the silent inquisition. I will no longer $\sqrt{}$, X, O, or abbrev. My name is Sam Levenson, not Levenson, Middle-name-if-any, None-if-none, Sam. My birthday, birth date, date of birth, day of birth are all December 28. I have no proof of birth except that I am alive and well and can write a full sentence. No, I will not print clearly, because I cannot print clearly above or below the line. Hand printing should be re-served for ransom notes. I may even write inside the box marked "Do not write in this box," because I never see the words "Do not write in this box" until I have already written in this box. You ask about my sex. Do I ask you? Whether my sex is "F, M, Other, None, Any," or "Last date of," is none of your business, and I will certainly not cross it out for anybody. I do not have a spouse. I have a wife. We do not have a marital status, just a double bed. My wife has no maiden name. She lost it on our wedding night along with some other personal effects. I, being more careful, still have my maiden name. You ask my "Father's age if living." If living, he would be one hundred and twenty-five. "Cause of his death?" Nothing serious. "Reason for request for birth certificate?" So that some day I may be eligible for a death certificate. If this is confusing, I suggest that you follow my final instructions, which are like those that come at the tail end of all your forms:

If answer to 5 is Yes, do not answer 4.

If answer to 4 is No, do not answer 3.

If 3 is already answered, proceed to 2.

Now add lines 2 and 5 and divide by 7, then put the answer below, above, next to, or under, but never inside the box marked "Strictly Confidential."

The questionnaire I find inside the carton of any new piece of equipment I have bought makes me uncomfortable. It implies that I have stolen the merchandise.

Where did you get this toaster? _____

When did you get this toaster? _____

Why did you get this toaster? _____

Who told you to get this toaster? _____

This last question implies that I have an accomplice. The next question implies that I am a second offender:

Is this the first time you have acquired our toaster? _____

The information-collector's job is to capsulize me, to bunch all my replies into a tentative profile, which is then inserted into an electronic wine press, which discards the pap of me and sends the rest on ahead through a fine electronic sieve, which rejects everything but what *it* considers to be me, which is finally converted into electronic impulses fed into an electronic computer, which in response to the finger-tip command of some anonymous clerk will "confidentially" reveal my essence to the world at large for a small rental fee.

Man, endowed with that incredible computer known as the human brain, has used it to invent an electronic brain that will protect him from the dangers of personal involvement. Electronic impulses prevent man from acting on human impulses. Except for the fact that the information we store in the machine may already be prejudiced or obsolete, the machine is assumed to be more objective, therefore more honest than man. It cannot be sentimental. (Tears rust the components.) Its mistakes, too, are superhuman. It would take fifty people working day and night for two hundred years to make the same mistake an electronic computer can make in two seconds.

To protect us from electronic invasion of our privacy the computers prefer to eliminate our names completely, granting us numerical anonymity and immunity. There is safety in numbers.

"Hello. I'd like to talk to 15452310450–Base 6."

"Sorry, you must have the wrong name. There is no one here by that number."

We are getting to the point where the man who is sent to jail will forfeit his number and be given a name to distinguish him from free men.

Man's days are numbered, and modern man, like his ancestors, will die when his number comes up.

The tombstones of national heroes may rate a few heart-felt words power-chiseled into the marble:

Here, subtracted from our total, lies one who amounted to much, respected alike by both numerator and denominator, a magnetic figure, dynamic in his impulses to the nth *degree, who will be mourned by all manpower.*

The grave marker of the mere mortal, however, will provide all the vital statistics necessary to preserve his memory:

HERE

TO THE BEST OF

OUR KNOWLEDGE

LIES

00017642/63/.04.

HATCHED 1910

MATCHED 1930

DISPATCHED 1973

XI

Meatballs vs Goofballs

⚘ ⚘ ⚘

I wonder if the synthetic, automatic, electronic world we are bequeathing to our children may not be at least partly responsible for sending them off on drug trips in search of lost senses buried, but possibly still alive somewhere, under layers of airproof, tasteproof, smellproof, touchproof ersatz abundance. We hardly dare ask our children any more to breathe deeply, to listen to the birdies singing (above the jet planes, automobiles, sirens, buses), to see the fishes in the (brown) brook, to taste the pretty (sprayed) apple, to look up at the (hazy) sunset. Their undernourished sense buds are dying on the vine. They are striving to reclaim sensation, to revive the message of sweet, sour, soft, hard, hot, cold, love, ah, ooh, and wow!

Many of them have obviously decided that they can rediscover their senses only by the use of drugs. They do not seem to be able to achieve "lightness of extremities," "floating on air," "quickened heartbeat," "joyous dreams," "euphoria," "tingling sensation," "feeling of peace," "intensified colors," "keener hearing," without the aid of horsepower, junk, LSD, morphine, goofballs, snow, speed, or ups. At the peak of our scientific sophistication they have returned to primitive witchcraft: bloodletting, skin-pricking, smoking of weeds, inhaling of magical vapors.

Are overdoses of drugs caused by underdoses of the joy of living? Children are born quivering bundles of sensation, exquisitely turned on. Yet in the prime of their youth they are pumping artificial ecstasy into their bloodstreams.

We cannot allow instinct to become extinct. We owe it to our children not to let their senses die. Sensitivity training begins at the mother's breast. What the child receives there does not have to be sterilized, homogenized, or warmed up. It feels good, smells good, sounds good, even looks good. It is close to the heart, and there are no sharp edges to hurt him. This is his first taste of love, and it will last a lifetime without artificial preservatives. Soul food starts here. Here, too, the sixth sense is born—call it empathy, sympathy, or love. Without it the other five senses do not really make sense. Without it we never really become fully human. Consciousness comes from the five senses; conscience from the sixth.

❁ ❁ ❁

The kitchen is the child's first school. There he will instinctively train himself for a lifetime of sensing. Show and Tell is for later. For now let it be Smell and Tell, Taste and Tell, See and Tell, Hear and Tell, Touch and Tell. Adults have only partial use of their senses. Kids use all of theirs in endless combinations. They will smell an onion, taste it, squeeze it, look at it, even listen to it. I have seen them chew a book, suck a pencil, kiss a pretzel, pat a puddle, lick a nickel, watch a flower grow, and soothe a broken heart by touching it with an old blanket.

Mothers can be pushers for some powerful sense experiences. At the risk of oversimplifying, I suggest that a kid raised in a bouquet of frying onions, sputtering chicken fat, or baking bread may never feel the need for sniffing glue. The American home does not need deodorizing. Right now it needs reodorizing. Bland, insipid cooking should be stamped "Unfit for Human Consumption." Food should be exciting enough to bring on "dilated pupils," "elation," "euphoria," "gasps," "spasms," "teary eyes."

Home is where the heart burns. In the hands of a talented food pusher meatballs can be as stimulating as goofballs. If enough of them are eaten late enough at night they will spark dreams. I know a bit about dreams, but I am an expert on heartburn. It is not a disease; it is a breathtaking experience. Despite much malicious propaganda, it is regarded by those of us who have been on intimate terms with it as a major source of unquenchable sense memories. Unless you can recall that middle of the night when the gush of cold seltzer hit the flame in your gut, you can lay no claim to familiarity with psychedelic phenomena.

A cold flat can be converted into a warm home with a pot of hot soup. It is an inexpensive type of central heating, and the varieties are infinite. I am a survivor of Mama's molten-lava treatment. One spoonful of her soup and I became a dragon, puffing smoke, some of it through my ears. I could feel the hot fluid mainlining it through my blood vessels, even into the fine capillaries of my eyeballs. If I ever made the mistake of trying to put out the fire by swallowing cold water, I found myself percolating. Between snorts and coughs I would express my admiration: "It's great [puff], Ma [puff]. It's great [puff]. Thanks [puff], Ma."

To a kid coming home from school there is no warmer reception than soup vapor spelling out "Welcome home!" Frozen foods can only spell "Come back later." I am not naïve enough to think that soup or meatballs is a cure-all for drug addiction. I cite them only as symbols of the relationship between child and home. They have a good moral odor.

There are bad moral odors, too, that affect our young. Many have been overexposed to the stench of ghettos, where they have been fed too long on the sense of hopelessness and lovelessness. These kids are not merely "underprivileged." They are Dead On Arrival. Cause of death: sniffing gloom.

Some addiction is born of contradiction. Too many of our wealthy young have been overexposed to the stench of expensive boredom, comfortable loneliness, leisure without purpose, in homes where people dwelled but never lived together, never really saw, heard, tasted, smelled, or touched each other. Life there made no sense.

And what about us elders who were brought up with the sweet old smells? Why is there so little euphoria in our crowd? We, too, have lost our senses. We are so wound up in our daily pursuit of a luxurious tomorrow that we cannot sleep tonight. We need nightly pill buttons to unwind us. We say we want to sleep. I'm not sure it is not amnesia we're after. Swallow an "Off" button and drop off. It's a great life if you don't waken.

The drug companies are more than willing to anesthetize us. They are the legal pushers and we are the legal users. "Are you suffering from 'simple nervous tension,' 'minor nervous tension,' 'occasional nervous tension'?" Here on the counter at your fingertips lies instant tranquillity. Try Dozo, Snoozo, Snoro, Dreamo, Nappo, Yawno, Zombo, or Damitol. In the morning you may need an "On" pill. Try Revivo, Returno, Socko, Adrenalo, or Combaco. Take the wrong pill and you may be brilliant all night and stupid all day.

In our pursuit of instant happiness we got hooked on television, booze, money, automation, cars, credit cards, synthetics, computers, telephones, which, instead of producing the hoped-for euphoria, have produced only the other effects of addiction: impaired judgment, panic, outbursts of temper, nightmares, paranoia, and delusions of grandeur. This is the grim world of the brothers happy.

Now may be the time to defrost the ideas and ideals of our early youth as a growing nation, to try to recapture those moments in our history when our senses were bursting with national pride. Perhaps we should retrace our steps to find out when, where, and, most important, why we lost our quickened heartbeat, tingling sensation, joyous dreams.

XII

He's a Sophomore

❀ ❀ ❀

Every family has its private jokes. If I say to Esther, "Don't worry. Just wait till the wrong girl comes along," she will laugh because she knows the lead lines: "I don't know what's the matter with my son," Mrs. Glott said to Mrs. Kotsch. "He's twenty-nine years old and not married yet!" "Don't worry, dearie, just wait till the wrong girl comes along."

If I say to Esther, "He's a sophomore," she will laugh. This story goes back to when we were at a wedding not long ago. I asked a friend, "What does the groom do for a living?" and she said, "He's a sophomore."

"He's a sophomore" is especially funny to us because I didn't ask Esther to marry me (nor she me) for about eight years. This was considered a sensible period to (1) get acquainted, and (2) get a job. A job was the first thing with which you went steady.

My preparation for marriage, however, started long before that. Since marriage was supposed to last a lifetime, the period of apprenticeship was long and arduous.

Like all other normal boys, I started at about the age of six by dipping girls' pigtails into school inkwells. By seven I was doing chalk murals on tenement walls of two hearts pierced by a single arrow discreetly signed with initials only: *S.L. loves Z.M.* By nine I was passing love notes to girls in class. Some notes were in code: "What's the answer to number 3?" meant "Will you meet me at 3 o'clock?" At the age of ten I went into my hate-girls period. I couldn't understand how boys of fourteen could love girls, and boys of fourteen couldn't understand how I could hate girls. Fortunately this stage lasted only a short while, and fortunately I had saved a couple of girls' names on a Like List so that if I ever stopped hating girls they would be the ones I would stop hating first. By thirteen I was writing real live love letters, committing myself to climb the highest mountains, swim the deepest rivers, and see you Saturday if it doesn't rain. On the back flap of envelopes I, like other young lovers, printed cryptic rubrics: SWAK, SWABK, SWAGBK, SWABBBK, SWL, SWLAK, SWAS, SWAH.

Girls often sealed these letters with a lipstick impression of upper and lower lips. Even if the letter, God forbid, fell into the hands of a mother she would never know that those secret symbols meant: sealed with a kiss, sealed with a big kiss, sealed with a great big kiss, sealed with a big, big, big kiss, sealed with love, sealed with love and kisses, sealed with a smile, sealed with a hug. An upside-down stamp meant "I love you."

I put one over on Mama when she intercepted a SWAK job I received in the mail.

"From who is this letter?"

"From my friend Harold."

"What's the red stuff on the back?"

"Harold must have cut his lip when he was licking the envelope, Ma."

"And what's the SWAK?"

"Oh, that? Hm. That, Ma? That, Ma, means Seasons Wishes and Kongratulations."

Walking down the street with a girl took courage. It meant you had turned traitor to the gang, and they let you know about it publicly. They lined the sidewalk as you passed.

"Hey, getta load of him! Look who's gotta girl!"

There was an implication, and they made it clear from the way they put their hands on their hips and wiggled their elbows and fannies, that your masculinity was suspect.

You could always save face by announcing, "It's my cousin." It was permissible for a boy to be seen in the company of a girl cousin. Girl cousins weren't really girls; they were just cousins. They didn't even look like girls. They were neuter. It could work the other way too. A girl was considered safe with a boy cousin. My mother once ordered me to take cousin Sophie to a school dance because her date had conked out. "Remember," Sophie warned me when we got there, "if anybody asks you, you're not a cousin, you're a boy. And don't forget, you're not here to enjoy yourself. You're here to dance with me!"

From about the age of eighteen on we courted in the damp hallways of the tenements, where love radiated more heat than the radiators. I got pneumonia twice in the same building. Our fiery breathing sent up clouds of steam, but not ever enough to defrost our extremities. The more aggressive swains would suggest one or two cozy undercover spots where bodily warmth could thaw a hand or two. "My hands are cold and it looks like nobody loves me." "God loves you and you can sit on your hands. I know you bought me a soda, but you don't have to try to squeeze it out of me." Their constant slapping of our hands and faces only raised our blood pressure and our interest.

We practiced mass courting. Privacy was unheard of. Each couple stood wrapped up in itself about three feet away from the next couple. Nonlovers and other transients maneuvered their way around us, discreetly ignoring our presence. It was not the normal flow of traffic that concerned us; it was the girls' irate fathers. Ten o'clock was curfew time. One second later a door was flung open and the voice of Father Time reverberated through the halls: "It's ten o'clock! Ruthie!" Ruthie cleared out so fast her beau was left kissing the letter boxes good-night. Shirley's father, himself an alumnus of the school of cold courting, once made a personal appearance in the hallway, his pants pulled angrily over long winter underwear, grabbed his daughter's terrified date by the shoulder, and yelled into his face: "Look, young feller. You wanna stand in the hallway with my Shirley, stand! But don't press her against the doorbells—you're waking up the whole building!"

Erotic fever could so overwhelm the affective cerebral areas that some temporarily insane swain might even venture a "Let's go upstairs." Girls knew that the best way to cool such ardor was to invite the boy upstairs. In many cases this first house call became the last. Going back a second time implied acceptance of the role of boyfriend, or steady, or regular, or fellow, or sweetheart. (For us "fiancé" was too ritzy and too foreign.) After that he was the leading man in the drama of marriage, morally committed to stay with the show from Act I, Scene I, through to the final curtain.

In most homes the kitchen was set aside as love quarters, a warm place where lovers could cook up large dreams on a small flame, a place where they were allowed to be together, but hardly alone. All around them were beds, beds, beds, occupied by people, people, people—mothers, fathers, brothers, sisters, snoring, moaning, muttering, tossing, but mostly listening, and they let you know they were listening.

"One little kiss, just one little kiss."

"Give him a kiss and let's get some sleep around here!"

"How can I ever leave you?"

"How's about a trolley?"

"I'd go through anything for you."

"How's about the door?"

We wooers were used to the heckling. What these wise-guys were doing to their sister at their house we were doing to our sister at our house. When my sister Dora walked into the kitchen with a suitor seven brothers hidden under quilts would sing out the *Lohengrin* "Wedding March" —"*Ta,* ra, ra, *ra!*" If he kissed her, we passionately kissed the backs of our hands—chmuck, chmuck, chmuck—or kissed each other loudly.

Papa was the least cooperative of all. This stranger had usurped his kitchen, the place where he drank his large glass of hot tea for two for one with lemon, at night. Papa was now a D.P. in his own home, sitting in his bedroom shivering in his smoking jacket (undershirt), waiting for the intruder to leave. Every fifteen minutes, like a cuckoo clock, Papa's head would pop out: "What time is it?" followed at irregular intervals with: "He's here yet? . . . He ain't got no home? . . . He's an orphan? . . . Whatsamatter it's so quiet? I don't like so quiet! . . . You're showing him the family pictures? Show him better the gas bills!"

Dora finally went back to the cold hallway mumbling, "At my wedding they ain't gonna sing 'Because'; they're gonna sing 'At Last.' "

❀ ❀ ❀

All mothers wanted their children to get married, but they set up a different timetable for each sex. Sons were always asked, "What's your rush?" and daughters, "What are you waiting for?"

Mothers never said they didn't like the girl. "I like that girl, Julius. She's a nice girl, a good girl, a sweet girl, a darling girl, but not for you. There are millions of girls who are for you. She's not one of them."

Daughters left their mothers to get married; sons left their mothers to join the enemy. "I finally worked him up to fifty dollars a week, so he gives it to a total stranger!"

While in theory he could choose the girl of his heart and she the boy of her heart, custom required that each had to please the hearts of his/her mother/father and the mother's/father's mother and father, and brothers/sisters, and relatives/friends on his/her side. The choice was free if ratified by the tribe.

It was not easy for a suitor to suit. If the papa liked him, the mama didn't; if the mama liked him, the papa didn't; if the mama and the papa liked him, the children didn't. By this time it was also possible that he hated their whole gang.

Giving the boy's line of work a classy title might swing family opinion in his favor. It was a game of seesaw. Every time the girl raised him up they knocked him down.

"He's a Marketing and Merchandising Promoter."

"He's a pushcart peddler?"

"He's with the government."

"He's a prisoner?"

"He's a Professional Fund Raiser."

"He's a pickpocket?"

"He follows the medical profession."

"He's an undertaker?"

One of the cleverest devices for silencing parental opposition was to label the choice as either "a girl like Mama" or "a boy like Papa." "A girl like Mama" conjured up an image of an immaculate Queen Mother and housekeeper. One of my brothers almost married a girl like Mama, but even Mama wouldn't let him. It was amazing. She looked like Mama, she talked like Mama, she dressed like Mama; she even looked older than Mama. One of the failings of girls like Mama was that they almost invariably looked like Papa. (The marrying-a-boy-like-Papa theory has been offered as an explanation of why mothers cry at weddings.)

A "boy like Papa" meant simply that he could be depended upon to be gripey, grumbly, and grouchy on the outside, but good, and tender, and noble on the inside. At least our Papa was. So Dora knew that Papa was only joking when he said: "You don't want to get married because you're our only daughter? And you don't want to leave Mama behind to take care of such a large family all by herself? Who are we to stand in the way of your happiness? You can take Mama."

XIII

Love, Shmove

It was hard to tell whether the papas and mamas of that era were happily married. The subject was not open for discussion, certainly not with their children.

"Are you happy, Ma?"

"I got nothing else to think about?"

Nobody had ever told Mama that marriage was supposed to make her happy; certainly Papa hadn't. Nobody had promised *him* happy either. Mature people prayed for good health, good fortune, and an honorable old age. A husband was supposed to make a living, and a wife was supposed to make a life of it. Only children talked of happiness; they still believed in fairy tales. Human beings, the old folks said, don't live happily forever after, most of the time not even during, so it was wise in marriage and in everything else to expect the worst. Then if it turned out to be only worse, it still wasn't too bad. Marriage was one of those things you were supposed to save for your old age, happy or not.

"Love, shmove!" Papa used to say. "I love blintzes; did I marry one?" The word "love" embarrassed them. It was an unmentionable, like "brassiere," "hernia," and "miscarriage." Not that they didn't believe in love. They felt it, but avoided the precise definition that young people demand. Defining it might lead to misunderstanding rather than understanding. Defining it might even diminish it.

To Mama love was not passion, or infatuation, or compatibility. She had given birth to ten kids without any of those. "Love," said Mama after many years of marriage, "is what you have been through with someone."

Love was made up of satisfaction ("Ten kids, thank God, is plenty"), sharing ("If he can take it, I can take it"), optimism ("Worse it couldn't get!"), and friendship, not in the style of Romeo and Juliet or Tristan and Isolde, but more like Damon and Pythias.

I knew my parents valued each other, because Papa told me always to listen to Mama and Mama told me always to listen to Papa; because whenever a decision was to be made regarding me, Mama said, "We'll ask Papa," and Papa said, "We'll ask Mama"; because Mama always watched at the window when Papa left for work and whispered to herself about his being "a good man, a learned man, to work so hard in a shop, it's a pity"; because at lunchtime she had me deliver a pot of hot soup two miles in the snow to Papa's shop so "he should know"; because Papa wouldn't spend a penny on himself unless Mama spent on herself. Share and share alike. So the day Mama had all her teeth pulled, Papa bought a suit.

If papas were at all romantic before marriage, they quickly shed "the foolishness" as soon after as possible. My father never took my mother out before they were married, and afterwards only if they were headed for the maternity hospital, which in Mama's case was often enough to give her rosy cheeks: "If it's nice out we'll walk; if it's raining we'll take an umbrella." They had never had a honeymoon: "We didn't have enough money, so Papa went by himself." There were anniversaries, but they went uncelebrated.

"How long are you married, Pa?"

"Please! Not while I'm eating!"

No candy, no flowers, no inscribed charms to wear on bracelets; nothing but a big, fat, immovable, indestructible wedding ring. The mamas believed that the best way to keep it bright and shiny was to soak it in hot soapy water several times a day. In a large family this was no problem. At the end of the day Mama could count on Papa to come home with those three little words on his lips that made it all worth while: "What's for supper?"

Every night, after we kids were in bed and supposedly asleep, I could hear Mama and Papa in the kitchen, not making love, no, but reading about it. Papa would read aloud the daily installment of a romantic novel that ran on forever in the Yiddish newspaper. He read in a dull, monotonous voice, perhaps to avoid betraying any emotional involvement in the subject matter, while Mama pressed his shirts, her tempo getting faster and faster as the story got hotter and hotter. The hissing of her iron seemed to become more urgent as the hero pressed his passion on the girl: ". . . and he drew her toward him, looking into the quivering pupils of her wide blue eyes and kissed her on her trembling lips—"

"Again?" said Mama, her iron coming to a dead stop. "He kissed her only yesterday!" Papa took a closer look at the paper and hurled it against the wall. "You're right! It's yesterday's paper!"

The day Albert and I caught Papa kissing Mama we got hysterical. "What happened, Al?" "I don't know. I think maybe the landlord died!" It had to be an event of supreme emotional significance. Papa had not kissed Mama even at their wedding. Theirs was a marriage of convenience between two poor families. The first time he had met her was at the wedding—and he would never kiss a girl the first time he met her! He certainly was not going to go around now kissing married women like Mama. (There was a religious custom of kissing your wife after twenty-four hours of fasting on Yom Kippur. It was not so much a kiss as a blessing.) Generally, kissing was considered unmanly. The presence of eight children had proved his manliness, but kissing, especially in the presence of eight children, was not the manly thing to do.

If any one of us tried to kiss Mama we would get brushed off with "Go away, crazy! You got nothing better to do?"— thereby classifying kissing as another of those "foolishness" things. Besides, it was dangerous to kiss Mama. She always wore a needle near the neckline of her dress, and a wild embrace could be fatal to the embracer. It was not the fashion of those times to smother children with kisses, but to smother them with care. I knew I wasn't being kissed, but I also knew I was being loved, even more than I deserved. It made one rise to the deserving.

We were living witness to love and marriage at its best and its worst: devotion, sacrifice, adoration, sympathy, loyalty, tenderness, along with anger, alienation, and bitterness. A loving couple and a quarreling couple could be one and the same couple. The secret of an enduring marriage was no secret. They quarreled. We saw nothing paradoxical about it. Married people exercised their marriages the way babies exercise their lungs, by yelling. They strengthened their matrimonial muscles by giving them a daily workout.

Psychiatrists do not look down upon the quarrel. Confrontation is also communication. The wide-open dialogue, the airing of the disparity between "is" and "ought," real and ideal, performance and aspiration, the itemized bill of particular offenses brought to the surface to be contested, denied, and sometimes admitted to, may have been (and may still be) my parents' version of today's encounter sessions.

They would rather fight than switch. Perhaps it was not even a fight. They cared enough for each other and for themselves to do battle with (rather than against) a worthy opponent. Perhaps they preferred discord over resolution. Perhaps they instinctively recognized that incompatibility was inherent in people and ideas, that dichotomy is really unity, that positives cannot live without negatives, and that opposites attract because they need each other. All of which, if true, led to the conclusion that if a man didn't have a wife, he would have to quarrel with total strangers, and for that they can take you away.

Like the sounds of slamming of doors, banging of pots, beating of rugs, and chopping of meat, the bickering of estranged bedfellows was an accepted household noise. ("Must you quarrel with me on the street? What do we have a home for?") Every room was a rumpus room. You could listen, but you must not interfere; it was dangerous. Either party or both could attack the peacemaker for "making trouble between us." (This has always been one of the occupational hazards of peacemaking.) Some quarrels started in the morning, were suspended when the man of the house left for work, and were resumed in the evening without missing a beat. Marital scraps, like food scraps, could be reheated. "He's home!" Evening events were the best. There was time enough for a fifteen-rounder.

We didn't need alarm clocks. The Kowalcik's gong rang at 6:00 A.M.; the Brown's at 6:30; the Michnik's at 6:45. If a morning fight ran on for a half hour or more it meant that the husband was sick and not going to work that day. ("God help me! I haven't got the strength for a sick man!") If there was no quarrel at all, Mama would worry: "It's been like that all day. What could it be? Sammy, go see if they are all right."

Those were our soap operas, not on the air but in it, all around us. We could tune in at any time and pick up snatches of dramatic dialogue. We knew the play; we knew the cast;

we knew the lines. But we never tired of them. Monogamy, yes; monotony, no.

Sometimes she talked first: "I don't understand you. Monday you liked fried herring, Tuesday you liked fried herring, Wednesday you liked fried herring, now all of a sudden Thursday you don't like fried herring!"

"Herring! Herring! It's not the herring! It's the last twenty years!"

Sometimes he talked first: "You can always leave me!"

"I'm gonna leave you and make you happy?"

There were attempts by the master of the house to prove he was master of the house: "You can hit me with that broom all you like; I'm still the boss in this house!"

The words "always" and "never" never failed to set off a violent emotional explosion.

"You always start a fresh bread."

"I don't always. Yesterday I didn't."

"You never talk to my mother."

"I don't always never talk to your mother—sometimes I forget not to."

There were accusations of the squandering of hard-earned money: "What did you do with the ten dollars I gave you on Friday?"

The answer came in two sizes:

Size 1: "What did I do with the ten dollars you gave me Friday? Oh, ho, ho! Wouldn't you like to know!"

Size 2: "So you want to know what I did with the ten dollars? So I'll tell you. A dollar here, a dollar there, is two dollars. You step in here and stop off there, is two more dollars—makes four, right? And before you can turn around two more dollars are gone—right? Makes six—good? And two dollars more for what you would never buy for me makes eight—right? And the other two? Oh, ho, ho—wouldn't you like to know!"

When words no longer sufficed to express the depth of their

anger they flew into a great silence, during which the children were used as messengers.

"Tell your father it's time to eat."

"Papa, Mama says it's time to eat."

"Tell your mother I'm not talking."

"Mama, Papa says he's not talking."

"So tell him 'Thank you'!"

"Tell her she's welcome."

A dying quarrel sometimes had to be revived. You can't quarrel alone: "I don't like the way you're sitting there not saying nothing."

On cold winter evenings, when the homework was finished and there wasn't much to do, the children could kindle a warm argument and huddle round it.

"Pa, Grandma said she never wanted Mama to marry you."

"*She* didn't want *me* . . . ?" And they were off.

My Uncle M. and Aunt N. hardly ever argued because they hardly ever talked to each other under the best of conditions. They produced five talkative, exuberant children in silence. Yet they never thought of leaving each other, because "people will talk."

The day Aunt N. got sick my brother Joe told Uncle M. to deliver Aunt N. to Mount Sinai Hospital in an ambulance. "I'll be waiting there for you under the main-entrance canopy." The ambulance pulled up, Uncle M. got out, but there was no Aunt N.

"Where's Aunt N.?"

"We had an argument, and she took the subway."

Years later, at Uncle M.'s funeral, Aunt N. stood at the graveside as they lowered the coffin, crying out: "Wait a minute! Listen! I want to talk to you."

As usual, he didn't answer.

It would seem that our constant exposure to the quarreling of the mamas and the papas might have turned us prematurely cynical. On the contrary, our early combat training taught us to bring our "as you like it" into focus with "like it is," not on the subject of marriage alone but on people partnerships in general. Even when we "played house" we didn't play like story-book princes and princesses but like real fighting people. "Look, you're only a prince. You can't be a king. You were king yesterday. I'm gonna be king. Okay, so get your own kingdom. You're banished anyhow."

We came to realize that every man and woman has something to say in his own defense; that there are not two sides to an argument, but dozens; that one of the reasons God said "Thou Shalt Not Kill" was that you might not yet have heard all sides of the story; that in human relations there is no perfect and final answer; that some ideas may never be happily wedded to others; that the dialogue, whispered or shouted, is eternal, and that the seeking of the answer is the answer.

We had absorbed a mature point of view: There's nothing wrong with marriage; it's just the living together afterward that's murder.

XIV

$E = MC^2$

❀ ❀ ❀

I was twenty-five years old before I had both job enough and courage enough to propose to Esther: "Marry me and you'll make me the happiest man on Saratoga Avenue between St. Marks Avenue and Prospect Place."

She came back with "I'll tell you the truth, Sam, I've already been asked to get married."

My heart fell to the ground dragging my knees along.

"You have? By whom?"

"By my mother and father—lots of times. I was just waiting for somebody besides them to ask me."

She reminded me that I was wearing a wristwatch she had given me that had been paid for by her father. It came with a card that read: "To Sam, On the Fifth Anniversary of His Engagement." (I bought her an engagement ring later—eleven years after we were married.)

She thought I ought to ask her father's permission. I knew that after thirty thousand house calls he was not likely to ask me, "Are your intentions honorable?" And I was too scared of him to come up with some crack like "You mean I have a choice?" So I got right to the point: "I've been going with your daughter for eight years . . ."

"So what do you want, a pension?"

He was trying to act like a tough father, which he could never do very well, but he was not going to surrender his only daughter to me without at least a token inquisition.

"Can you support a family?"

"I wasn't thinking of that yet, but . . ."

"I just wanted you to know that there are four of us, not counting my wife's father, who lives here too."

"I'll tell you the truth—I was planning on her alone."

"Would you marry her even if she didn't have a penny?"

"I certainly would!"

"Well, you're a lucky boy. You got the right girl."

We chose the twenty-seventh of December to get married, because I was now teaching school and it came right in the middle of the first paid holiday of my life. Once we had chosen the date, however, our choices were done with. From that point on tradition took over.

Tradition required that all joys and sorrows be shared, that marriage, like birth and death, be treated as a communal sacrament, one in which God and man were involved. This solved the problem of whom to invite to the wedding—God and the immediate family of man.

Poor people traditionally made large weddings. The poorer, the larger. The more people, the richer the experience. Esther and I discussed, in secret of course, the possibility of a poor but small wedding, but this was too revolutionary an idea for our elders to understand, so we made it large but intimate. Tradition required that we please our parents, and it did not displease us to do so.

We fought for and won a concession on their part, a live

violin-piano-cello trio to play Schubert, because his melodies were plaintive enough to pass as Jewish.

We had one great advantage over other couples. Esther and I are second cousins and members in good standing of the Yoseph Chonah Family Circle, Inc. We therefore did not have to send out invitations. We simply notified the recording secretary of the organization to announce the wedding at the bottom of the regular meeting notice next to "Dues, Arrears, and Fines."

Since there was no other side of the family, we were spared the sinking feeling that so many people experience when they go to a wedding and see "them," that strange bunch on the other side of the aisle. Wedding guests divide themselves instinctively into two groups and stare at the other "them." Even though they have not yet met, they already regard each other with tribal suspicion. Our side is always nice, good-looking—but them! "Did you see *them*? Oh, boy, what we fell into!"

Ours was a totally we-sided wedding, all intelligent and attractive. They looked at and looked like each other on either side of the aisle, and were pleased with what they saw. "Such a lovely family, and such a beautiful couple, especially her."

The Yoseph Chonah Family Circle, Inc., our Cousins Club, named for a common great-great-grandfather, Yoseph Chonah, from whom we had all descended (some a bit lower than others), had been established by our foresighted elders as a bulwark against the disintegration of the family. Brotherhood through cousinhood! They wanted us to get to know our ancestors both living and dead. For the living they had monthly meetings in a rented meeting hall; for the dead they acquired a permanent clubhouse—a family cemetery plot.

"We should stand together in this world and lay together in the next."

The first cemetery committee (the "burypickers" we called them), consisting of the eldest of the elders ("What do these young snotnoses know about dying?"), men who were well on their way to where we were all going, went out to dig up a place "for the entire body." They never came back. The younger cousins suggested that they must have been looking over a model grave and fallen in, or that, at their advanced age, they felt it was hardly worth going back and forth.

The second cemetery committee did return with lots of dust from the land of to-dust-returnest in their pants cuffs, a skeleton plan in their hands, and a report: "Fellow cousins, it's out of this world. It's near a subway, a short walk from a synagogue and a movie, a view that will take your breath away. Nice and dry if, God forbid, you have rheumatism, and not near poison ivy, you should have to scratch away the rest of your life. And immediate occupancy."

There were some touchy problems about burial protocol.

"Let's open with the president and his wife," the snotnoses suggested. The presidential couple declined the honor.

"Maybe in alphabetical order?" caused Uncle Aron to resign from the organization, especially since he was listed on the membership rolls with two *a*'s—"Aaron."

"For goodwill, how about we give two graves for a wedding present?"

"Once you die you don't have to pay no more dues."

"But suppose a member dies with his dues behind?"

A stern statement of burial policy was written into the constitution by the elders.

Article I, Burial: Who Is Eligible:
Only members in good standing are eligible for burial. Be it herewith known that any member who shall owe to the

Cemetery Fund a sum in excess of three dollars ($3.00) will not only not be interred but shall be **IMMEDIATELY** ejected from the organization—after being sent a Registered Letter sixty days after a previous notice of removal, and he/she shall be allowed ninety days in which to pay back dues.

If said debt is not paid up within one year, a six-month period will be allowed for appealing the case to the Executive Board. If delinquent member should die in the meantime, an additional two months will be allowed. Under these conditions a member may be expelled from the cemetery **WITHOUT NOTICE.**

Be it also known that all members must decease within city limits. If not, they will have to be bused at their own expense to the New York side of the George Washington Bridge, where the Y.C.F.C. will pick up the obligation.

Uncle M., the chairman of the Funeral Arrangements Committee for some thirty years, takes care of all the details, including the selection of what he insists on calling "a box."

"Hello. I. J. Morris Funeral Parlors? Jerry? Listen, Jerry, this time we want a box that should last a lifetime. His wife didn't like the last one. One good wiggle and he's out in the cold. We have another event for you for this Sunday. Yes, the usual package deal—box, service, and hearse. Put an ad in the paper: 'The Y.C.F.C. mourns the loss of loyal friend, brother, father, partner, brother-in-law, father-in-law, grandfather, grandfather-in-law, former president of the Y.C.F.C. Services at 2:00 P.M. sharp. In case of rain after 12:00 noon, services will be held at 9:00 A.M. the same morning, rain or shine.'"

Our funerals are well attended. This makes the elders very happy. "We should do this more often and really get to know each other."

Any member who is moved to do so can walk up to the coffin and say a few heartfelt words, and they do: "Cousins, what you see before you here now is only the shell; the nut is gone."

When our Cousins Club reached its tenth anniversary it decided to celebrate by doing something special. They appointed me general chairman. I tried to come up with some thrilling surprise, so I wrote a letter to a man I knew they all revered and offered him honorary membership in our family circle. I explained the background so that he would know what he was getting into if he were to accept. To my own amazement and the utter disbelief of all my relatives, I received the following reply (the original hangs on my office wall):

My dear Mr. Levenson:

It gives me pleasure to accept the honorary membership of your family circle. Send, if possible, greetings to my newly aquired [sic] honorary great-grandfather.

Sincerely yours,

(signed) Prof. Albert Einstein

Our women sent Cousin Albert several jars of homemade pickled herring, but we never heard from him again. He died in Princeton, New Jersey, beyond our jurisdiction.

All members of the Y.C.F.C. came to my wedding, even those behind in their dues, because the rites required their presence and because they had the right to be there, a traditional relatives' right guaranteed by some pre-Einsteinian theory of relativity to the effect that any relative of any mother of mine was a relative of mine into infinity. $E = MC^2$: Everybody is my mother's cousin twice removed.

This was not an era of come-to-the-wedding-as-you-are. My people came cleansed, purified, and anointed, as befitted a sacred occasion. They had religiously scoured away the tiniest particles of the profane—specks of paint, dough, plaster, and other stains of their daily lives. The men had shaved their beards past the roots into the blood vessels. Some still carried bits of toilet tissue glued to cuts, powdered over heavily, giving their faces the appearance of carnival masks. The daughters who knew about beauty parlor beauty had glamorized their mamas, weaving their hair into queenly patterns, pulling their corsets tight enough to keep their lips and cheeks blue-blooded for the evening, maneuvering them into youthful gowns, forcing their matronly feet into Cinderella-size shoes, and finally presenting them at the ball to be admired, if not recognized. "That's Aunt Jennie?" Brothers had to take a second look at their sisters. "You look so beautiful I didn't recognize you."

"Thank you!" Not to be recognized was the highest compliment.

Since relatives were plentiful and money was scarce, and since the estimated cost of wedding pictures was a bit higher than the estimated cost of feeding our esteemed relatives, and since the musical trio was already running into overtime even before half the guests had arrived, we decided to pose for just one picture (which we would buy later "if we like it"). Since there is something about memory that makes images more rather than less vivid with time, especially if the original is done in loving color, and since the people present that night were not passersby but permanent residents in our life, we have never really missed the photos.

We didn't even buy the one wedding picture we had offered to buy if we liked it. "Mr. Bluebird" of Bluebird Studios on Pitkin Avenue even put it in the window to tempt us. We often went there to look at it. Later on we even took Conrad to see it. By the time we could afford to like it, the picture had faded and "Mr. Bluebird" had lost the negative.

What we finally got was a picture of a faded picture made from a negative made from a picture. Our wedding picture ended up looking very much as we do now.

I could have predicted the fate of our wedding picture. Life with Mama was picturesque, but we had very few pictures to prove it. Besides it was cheaper for Mama to display kids than pictures. We each looked like each other or like Mama or Papa, so how many pictures did we need? "He's the picture of his father."

Mama's and Papa's wedding picture has gotten lost. I don't know where it is, but I do know what it is. I stared at it for long periods when I was a child. It was a picture not just of two people but of the institution of marriage in their time. It was earnest, determined, stoic. Against a backdrop of what looked like a castle, or a penitentiary, in what looked like an electric chair sat Papa, stunned, staring straight ahead, his hands gripping the arms of the seat, ready for the blindfold, resigned to the verdict of matrimony about to be passed on him. Next to him, standing, was the bride, looking already like Mama, in her upholstered dress, her consoling hand resting on the doomed man's shoulder, chaplain style, a gold watch suspended from a chain around her neck ticking off the moments left to him. Papa already had the look that was to stay with him through the years, the look of hope for a last-minute reprieve.

If a photograph, as it is said, can capture a moment of life, those two sure looked captured for life! Papa said years later in one of his rare moments of humor that if he had known we were coming, he would have gone through with the execution.

Our wedding ceremony did not require a rehearsal. The old-timers knew the traditional rites—not only what was right but the rights of each within the rites.

The ceremony started late, but the crying started early. It was traditional to cry at joyous occasions, especially for women who were specialists in heartache. The men did not cry, they just blew their noses very loudly. Those who couldn't blow coughed, sneezed, belched, or gasped for breath. Some were so overcome they loosened their ties, belts, and shoelaces to keep from fainting. The tears were partly superstition, not letting on to evil spirits (and possibly evil men) that Jews were having a celebration and where they were having it; but mostly the tears came from a disbelief in the possibility of pure joy in human life, a belief in fact that life and death are one, that one will not come to a party without the other, and that death might be temporarily placated if honored by an open invitation rather than having him show up in a huff at the height of the festivities to demand the homage due him.

Besides, they loved us. What better way for them to show love than to cry, not near us, but on us, unashamedly letting their hot teardrops run down our necks like a broken necklace of warm wet pearls, into our collars, down into our underwear, literally pouring affection upon us. Tears were not in bad taste, nor did they really taste bad. These people, like their tears, were the salt of the earth, and while there was much pathos in what they were doing, they were not pathetic. "Sammy, our Sammy, our Esther, our little Sammy. Remember when I held you in my arms?" I couldn't remember, because I was three weeks old at the time, but I said I did. This released a new flood of tears, and a new set of memories of my achievements, which I could not remember because they had never happened, but I acknowledged them all: the medals, the good deeds, the brilliant scholastic record, the violin recitals, the sick uncles I had sat with. Who was I to diminish their love for me or to deny these poor people the luxury of a rich cry? What's a wedding without tears? A dehydrated affair at best.

Everybody participated in the ceremony, either by marching down the aisle or by crying on either side of it. The elders were given the privilege of walking down the aisle first, in twos in the style of the guests in Noah's Ark, one of each gender, a grandpa and a grandma, a father and a mother, an uncle and an aunt. Anybody coming down the aisle was greeted with a mass clearing of sinuses. There were enough tears for all, including the caterer, who was busy taking a house count for the fruit cups.

They wept at our two-year-old flower girl, her soaking-wet lace panties slipping lower and lower down her legs with each step forward, her big black eyes kept wide open by the black coffee her grandmother had fed her to keep her awake. She came down the aisle in a trance, throwing roses before her and stepping on them all the way down the aisle.

"Gorgeous! Gorgeous!"

They wept when cousin Frances sang "Because you come to me . . ."

"He came to her! How well I know! Wasn't I there!" Sniff, sniff, sob, sob.

The rabbi in his flowing black robe brought on general hysterics. They remembered him from the Y.C.F.C. funerals. "Him! God help us! I need air!"

Esther was a smash. They stood up to call out their tearful admiration for every detail. "Such a gown!" Sniff. "Such a face!" Blow. "That's an Esther like from the Bible an Esther." Shlip, shlop. "Did you ever?" Shlop, shlip. "No, I never!"

The major celebrants of the ritual were now all gathered under the canopy. Step by step the rabbi proceeded to marry us. He told us why we were there, read the marriage certificate first in Aramaic then in English, welcomed us unto the House of Israel, had me say the Hebrew equivalent of "With this ring I thee wed," told us to go forth and multiply, had me offer to share my worldly goods (my worldly what?) with my bride, had us sip wine from the same goblet, had us lower our heads and pronounced the ancient priestly blessing upon us: "May the Lord bless you and keep you, may the Lord let His countenance shine upon you and be gracious unto you, and bring you peace." Then, our heads still bowed, he went on to: "O God, full of compassion, Thou who dwellest on high! Grant perfect rest beneath the sheltering wings of Thy presence, among the holy and pure who shine as the brightness of the firmament, unto the soul of the departed Rebecca Levenson, who has gone into eternity. Lord of mercy, bring her under the cover of Thy wings, and let her soul be bound up in the bond of eternal life. Be Thou her possession, and may her repose be peace. Amen."

I didn't know whether tradition or Papa had called for it, but there it was, a prayer of mourning for Mama, who was no longer with us. My brothers and sister knew that Mama was the bond that tied us all together. Yet none of us, not even Papa, had had the courage to mention the word "Mama" that day. It was Papa who had asked for the prayer. Was it possible that after all these years he was declaring his love for Mama, that his public "love shmove" was only a cover-up for his private embarrassment? I left my bride, walked over to Papa, and put my arms around him. He kissed me for the first time in my life, and we broke into tears. We, who had hardly ever talked together, were now crying together.

We had walked together once. Neither of us had forgotten.

It was shortly after my Bar Mitzvah. Papa and I were alone in the house the day Mama died. It was Friday morning, always a stressful time for a Jewish woman, who had to purify her home for the arrival of the Sabbath, which they called "the Bride." Death knew where to find Mama any Friday morning—on her knees washing the floor. And that was where she died. Following ancient orthodox ritual, a group of elderly women were called in to wash Mama's body and put her to rest on the floor, some candles near her head.

After the family was called together (brother Joe, the doctor, signed her death certificate), she was placed in a hearse, which carried her to the steps of Papa's synagogue, from which the rabbi wailed some verses beseeching God's mercy. The hearse then proceeded down the block. No one told us to, but we did what we had seen done before. Tradition. We lined up behind the hearse in a funeral cortege, Papa and I first, behind us the family.

It was summer. The sun was shining. I could not understand how the sun could shine in such darkness. Birds sang gayly from the telephone wires. I hated the sunshine and I hated the birds. The sidewalks were lined with neighbors, mostly women in their stained aprons also caught in the middle of preparing for the Sabbath, knowing they had been spared for now, sobbing and pointing at me: "Left over, a child, a child, a child." As I walked behind the slowly moving black wagon, my head bowed down, I saw fragments of my childhood coming toward me from between the wheels, chalk drawings of hearts, baseball bases, boxes for hopscotch, crisscrosses of ticktacktoe, parts of tops and checkers. Out of nowhere, or perhaps from somewhere where the sun had some reason to shine and birds to sing, a rubber ball came bouncing between the wheels. It hit the inside of one wheel and was sent spinning against the opposite wheel, back and forth, picking up momentum with each bump, seeming to be not only unaware of danger but leaping back again and again for more, taunting the wheels. Then at the height of its joyousness a soft pop, a squish, and it lay there baby pink on the inside, gashed on the outside. Its last breath rose gently to my nostrils. It was the smell of death. I knew that the time had come for me to put away the things of my childhood. That day I became a man.

At the funeral brother Mike dropped some petals on Mama's pinewood coffin. Flowers at a funeral were against tradition, but no one objected, not even Papa.

When we got home, one of the neighbors brought out a pitcher of water. Tradition. We washed death off our hands and went back to life. Sister Dora turned to Albert and me. "You'll have to be good on your own now. Nobody's ever gonna yell at you again." She asked us all to wait while she went into the house and finished washing Mama's floor.

Papa wrote the inscription for the tombstone: INSEPARIBLE IN LIFE AND DEATH.

Misspelled forever.

I left Papa still crying and went back to complete the wedding ceremony, which from this point on became inaudible because of the mass lamentation in the hall. Even the trio was crying. There was only one more ritual act left for me to perform, to smash a small wine glass under my heel as a reminder again of the fragility of human happiness. I pulverized the glass with one loud scrunch, the drummer hit the cymbal, and joy took over. Mazel tov! Mazel tov! Mazel tov! Mazel tov! . . . The musicians caught the beat, and the crowd was off and dancing in the aisle before we could make our way back.

It was not the young but the old who were the first to kick up their heels, reverting instinctively to the dances of their youth. Off they went in a mad whirl, squaring circles, circling squares, spinning wildly clock- and counterclockwise, in twos and threes, changing partners, changing color, their blood pressures soaring through their varicose veins, corsets bursting, pants splitting, trusses slipping, beads spilling, shoes flying. While the young clapped for them, they polka'd, mazurka'd, hopaked, czardas'd, waltzed, hora'd, or just held on to each other for dear life, for sweet life, for good life, for life, for life, L'chaim! L'chaim!

The young watched in fascination as some of their elders tried once again to become flirting beaus and coy damsels doing courting dances, gleams in their eyes shining through their cataracts. "Remember, Sarah?"—and he poked her lasciviously while the children screamed.

The trio switched to a march whose message was clear: Dinner. The guests lined up in couples and paraded around the room in courtly fashion, the ladies holding the elegantly raised elbows of their escorts with the tips of their fingers as though they were gentlemen rather than husbands.

In the dining room the president of the Y.C.F.C. called for a roll on the drum, made a short speech, and handed over an envelope containing our wedding present: a gift certificate for two graves.

We were married in Brooklyn. For our honeymoon we went to Manhattan, by subway, to the Sheraton Hotel, where for $3.75 a night we were given a large bedroom with two beds. Wow! Two beds! My bride had the opposite reaction. "Oh no, oh no!" She turned toward the wall and began to cry.

I couldn't understand. "What's the matter? Isn't it nice?"

"It's very nice, but I thought we were going to have the room all to ourselves!"

Our honeymoon was traditional.

In the morning we had room service. I went to the nearest grocery man, bought an order of lox, bagels, cream cheese, and milk, and we served ourselves in the room. What we didn't finish we put out on the cold windowsill, as all married people did.

XV

AWOL

❀ ❀ ❀

People are still marrying for better or for worse, for richer or for poorer, but not for long. It is still true that lots of people can't live without each other—until they get married; then they can. (United we stand; but separated we can stand it even better.) The trend indicates that marrying the one you love is much easier than loving the one you married, and that constancy in marriage is much harder than constantly getting married. In this era the happiest days of a woman's life are her wedding days, and afternoon weddings are the happiest of all. If it doesn't work out, she hasn't killed the whole day. "I do" and "Adieu" are running neck and neck.

It is no longer death but life that parts. The split-level marriage (living in one place and loving in another) is becoming not only more common but more commonly accepted. It is not easy to cast stones at people who are always on the move between bed and board. All attachments (romantic as well as electronic) now come with a long extension cord that can be plugged in anywhere. Everybody's gone AWOL—Away on Love. The bluebird of happiness lives away from home. There have been several attempts (all failures) to compile a *Who's Whose in America.* Everybody's making house calls but doctors. Perhaps it's only a liberal interpretation of the injunction "Love thy neighbor."

In marriage as in everything else it is getting harder to get things repaired or even to get replacements for the parts that have worn out. Get a new one. Couples now would rather switch than fight. That's the new happy ending. Whatever the causes may be, love and marriage no longer seem to go together like a horse and carriage, or is it that the age of the horse and carriage was a better age for marriage? Or is it that horses, carriages, and marriages have all become obsolete at the same time?

Whatever the causes may be, one giant-size paradox confronts us at the moment: Since people started to marry for love and love alone, as free men should (not like Mama and Papa), and started to settle their differences reasonably, as free men should (not like Mama and Papa), the rate of broken marriages has accelerated. Even broken marriages are not doing well, and the partners often have to get together again.

For many of our young marriageables wedlock is on the way out. They are conscientious objectors to all locks. Even a simple gold wedding band may cut off the circulation.

Grandpa said, "love, shmove" but got married. His grandson prefers unbridaled, free-lance love. He loudly proclaims his affection for girls and his disaffection from marriage. He wants all the fringe benefits, but won't join the union. "I don't want a marriage license," he says (and she nods), "your hypocritical scrap of paper, the lease you matrimonial slumlords want me to sign so I can live in a decrepit institution unfit for human habitation." (She nods again.) "Either you renovate, remodel, or rebuild or we don't move in." (Nod, nod, nod.)

"As for the marriage vows you choose to demean into a business contract, we will accept them if we must, but only with all the protective clauses found in other commercial deals of your establishment. We want them on approval, renegotiable upon the demand of either party, with marital satisfaction guaranteed or premarital status cheerfully returned. We do not want to live in the hallowed halls of marriage forever after. We want only visiting privileges.

"We cannot take vows based upon forever-after, since we do not believe in forever-after any more than we believe in the heretofore or the hereafter. All our beliefs are *pro tem* or *ad hoc*. This makes all our commitments tentative, including marriage. All bonds should self-destruct before bondage sets in."

Our young are considerate of our feelings and do not attack our marriages on a personal basis. We are good people, our children concede, but we are cowardly. We set a bad example by compromising with life. We accepted the possible. We should have held out for the possibility of the impossible. If marriage is not the original sin, staying married under anything less than a permanently ecstatic alliance is equivalent to living in sin.

The new marriage mores seem like home movies of the old ways run off backwards. Everybody seems to be backing down the aisle, away from the altar rather than toward it.

Sleepy or not, more and more parents are having the new bedtime story read to them by their children.

"Yes, Mother, we're living together. You wouldn't want us to be dishonest, would you, Mother? We love each other. If you love each other and don't live together, that's dishonest. We're not ready to be married; we're only ready to be honest.

You wouldn't want us doing it behind your back, Mother; that wouldn't be honest. You and Daddy weren't honest. Physical love between consenting partners is honest, so why don't you and Daddy consent?" (With parental consent they can get a learner's permit.)

Parents who cannot honestly take all this honesty are left with two alternatives: (1) to make a scene, which ends in the child's moving out, or (2) not to make a scene, which also ends in the child's moving out.

The cohabit habit is becoming a life style with clear advantages, such as an unlimited number of honeymoon trips on a student discount.

While the children are away premaritalizing, the parents have a chance to discuss things in the kid's empty bedroom.

"Let's talk it over, darling. They're gonna do it anyhow. If anybody asks us, we'll say they're engaged. If they ask, 'Engaged in what?' we can say they are studying together, sort of cramming for their Wassermann test. Since they are both at Yale, they want to try it out in New Haven before they bring it into a legitimate house in New York.

"You never say they are having an affair. That's old-fashioned. They are having a relationship. He's a sort of sleep-in friend. No, we can't call him our son-in-law. He's our friend-in-law. Let's be modern. More and more college students are marrying their roommates."

Our friend the sophomore is not saying, "I want no part of your marriage mores." No. He is saying, "I'll pick the parts I like."

His wedding rites are now part of his civil rights. Even the nonradical young have made some radical changes.

"This is the ceremony we're going to have, Mother. No aisle. Aisles represent the rigid unilateralism of tradition. Just a circle of friends seated on the grass in the park at dawn, with lighted candles in their hair, humming mystic hymns to the first rays of the rising sun as they strike the motorcycle

157

reflectors. I shall lead my bride to the public fountain, symbol of Aquarius, from which we shall both drink. Then we'll chant our vows in unison: 'Out of two, one, and never none nor ever more nor less than all, borne by the river of time to the seventh power of nine lotus petals reposing on the eternal pools of limpid unity.' Then I shall sprinkle some symbolic unbleached organic wheat germ on her breasts, and we shall be man and wife."

Patiently, lovingly, his mother pleads for her past while he begs to bypass it.

"But where does our family fit into this field day?"

"The family is an outmoded social organism, Mother."

"Is that a nice way to talk about your relatives?"

"For me relatives are people I relate to, Mother, and I do not relate to those people."

"How come you are old enough to have relations but not relatives?"

"My family is not necessarily my next of kin. We don't believe in chromosomal chauvinism."

"Daddy will be heartbroken if he can't march down the aisle with you."

"Marching is militaristic."

"Okay, so we'll call it a peace march. And how about Grandma? What's her part?"

"We respect her, but she's too ethnically parochial for the world of tomorrow. Her ancestors are Abraham, Isaac, Jacob, Moses, and Isaiah; ours are Paine, Jefferson, Lincoln, Freud, Marx, and Einstein."

"Look, if you can invite your friends, we can invite ours. Are you sure God will be present?"

"Only as a transcendental spirit, not as an anthropomorphic projection of primitive man."

"Okay, so he's a spirit. But man does not live by spirit alone. Who's going to do the catering?"

"We abhor the killing of animals, Mother."

"But a little vegetarian chopped liver made with mineral oil can't offend your religious beliefs."

"Okay, if it's in the shape of a dove."

"And how about a little music? It's a wedding. People will want to dance."

"Just a harmonica and a zither."

"How about a rabbi?"

"Only if he has no religious hangups."

"No girl to sing 'Because you come to me . . .'?"

"Male chauvinism, Mother."

"And no little flower girl?"

"Adult chauvinism, Mother."

"And a ring?"

"Slave symbolism, Mother."

"At least you're going to break the glass!"

"In my bare feet?"

"By the way, we haven't met her parents yet. Are they coming?"

"Look, Mother, it's a small wedding. You have to draw the line somewhere."

"How come you didn't feel crowded in at Woodstock?"

"It was our crowd, Mother."

"Are you going on a honeymoon?"

"Yes. To Russia."

"What a coincidence."

"What do you mean?"

"That's where your grandfather ran away from when he was your age. Look, let's compromise. Maybe we can put yours and ours together. Okay, no aisle; just a green runner, with relatives on either side. Our circle of friends couldn't sit on the grass in a circle. It would be hard for them to get up again. No candles in their hair either. Just enough love in their hearts to light your way as you pass, like you say, down the river of time.

"Daddy and I would like to get dressed up. For us this is a

very big happening. You've got *your* beads; we have *ours*. We like to cry at weddings; let us. We like to remember the dead; let us. We like to bless the bread and the wine, and the ring; let us. We've got rights too. We like that 'out of two, one' stuff. When you say 'I do' or 'I hope so' or 'I'll do my best,' there will no longer be two sides here, but one—out of two, one. You believe in peace; so do we. And for making peace there's nothing like chopped liver. It can be shaped into a dove, or a heart, or even a dove with a heart. Yes, my son, even a dove needs a heart. A wedding is a feast. Let all who are hungry for love or food come and share with us. Everybody's invited!"

"Sounds great, Mother, but I'll have to ask my bride."

"Now, that's tradition!"

"That's what?"

❁ ❁ ❁

My sophomore looks askance upon tradition. He does not recognize its authority. He is the author of his own authority. The test of truth, like the Rorschach test, is what he sees in it. He cannot be flunked on a morality test, since morality is no longer absolute.

"If it's good for me, that's good enough for me. If I like it, it is right. There is no undesirable behavior. If I desire it, now, under these circumstances, it is desirable."

"You make your own moral judgments, young man? Aren't you pretending to moral infallibility?"

"No. I pretend only to being alive by divine right."

"Does that also mean that you are right by divine right?"

"If I am true to myself, I become infallible for myself."

"Isn't it possible that what you are calling self-determination is nothing more than an alibi for the sin of self-indulgence?"

"There is no sin greater than the sin of self-denial."

"How about the rights of others?"

"All have the same right—to be themselves."

"How about a sacred code like the Ten Commandments?"

"You kept them not because they were sacred but because you were scared."

"That may be; but we kept them."

"Not in very good condition. They have disintegrated because of all the loopholes you drilled into them. You are not as much of a conformist as you pretend."

"At least we have a set of moral precepts to live by."

"Do you really mean moral precepts or a list against which to check your transgressions?"

"How can you have a morality with no 'nots' at all?"

"We pick our 'shalts' and 'shalt nots.' "

"You can't go on choosing the parts of the Ten Commandments you like, this from Column A and that from Column B. Sounds like a menu."

"Right again. We follow our appetites."

"Are there no bad appetites?"

"If nature provides the appetites, we shall provide their satisfaction."

"In other words, your ethics serve the needs of your bodies."

"Right again. The lust for life is a moral imperative. We follow our instincts, and sex is the most imperative. We can't wait."

XVI

It's Better If You Wait

❁ ❁ ❁

The sex education we got at home was as negative as our marriage education was positive. Not only do the young today know more about sex than I did when I was their age, they know more at their age now than I know at my age now. And when they tell me, I still don't fully understand. The incredible is not easily comprehensible.

The "facts of life" were kept from me as long as possible on the assumption that the less I knew, the less chance I had for getting into trouble. Fig leaves were placed over the two most vulnerable parts of my body—my ears and my eyes. Hear no evil. See no evil. "Speak no" was added to "Hear no, see no." If I even looked as if I might ask where I came from, they washed my mouth with soap. "He's gonna ask again! Here comes Dirty Mouth. Quick, the soap!" I got the idea that babies came from soap.

My parents had never heard of Freud. In our building there was one Fried, one Freund, and two Friedmans, but not one Freud. How could I expect parents who blushed at the word "love" to talk of sex? Sex was mentioned on birth certificates, but never brought up again. If in the course of their conversation they came to some word that "it's better he shouldn't know," their eyes turned to me and their tongues turned to Russian. Those are the only Russian words I know. If I ever visit Moscow, they're going to wash my mouth.

Mama used one acceptable four-letter word. It was supposed to act as a contraceptive against four-letter deeds. The word was *"don't."* Even when pronounced "mustn't," "oughtn't," "dasn't," or "shouldn't," it still came to that fearletter word: *"don't."* A clean mind in a clean body: for the mind *"don't";* for the body soap. The idea of forbidden fruit didn't make me feel particularly deprived. Premarital sex was only one more of the items we were forbidden to taste, along with pork, scaleless fish, and meat from animals without a cloven hoof. It just wasn't kosher.

With time the fig leaves got dry and curled a bit at the edges. I saw even if I didn't look; I heard even if I didn't listen. I could even whisper a suspicion or two, but real answers were still not forthcoming.

"When you'll be as old as I am you'll know," Papa would say.

By that time I'd be more interested in where I was going than where I came from. The fact that you wanted to know didn't seem important to Papa. "So he wants to know. So what? You have to give him everything he wants? Next he'll want a bicycle!"

The stork story made no sense to me. I could not conceive of any stork dragging eight kids up six flights of tenement stairs. Besides, if a stork ever showed up at our house, Mama would have plucked him and cooked him. If there were any unhatched eggs in the stork's interior, Mama would, as usual, have fed them to my sister. She always did it with unhatched chicken eggs. It was some sort of fertility rite for daughters only. As a mother of eight kids, she probably figured the less she fertilized her sons, the safer other mother's daughters would be.

Of all the "facts" that I picked up, the truth was the one I refused to accept. I couldn't believe the terrible things *they* were saying about *my* mother and *my* father. Maybe my father, but not my mother.

I looked for clues in the Bible. While the Good Book recorded generations and generations of who begat whom, it never mentioned how. "He was *with* her" or "He *knew* her" didn't help me at all. I *knew* my Uncle Louie and was *with* him a lot. So?

On the advice of our resident ten- or eleven-year-old sex-perts we turned to such books as the dictionary to break the adult code of sexual silence. Certain words had already been underlined by other researchers. Hidden behind some very innocent-looking words was the real lowdown. No cabalist ever delved more deeply into hidden meanings, implications, or concealed truths than we did. "Look up 'friction,' kid." Our fingers and our imagination ran feverishly through "friction," "intervene," "splice," "cul de sac," "prostration," "interpolate," "savoir faire," "abreast," "junction," "inter-ject," "intermediary," "dovetail" . . . (I do not intend to de-prive the reader of the fun of looking up the definitions for himself.)

Visual aids for the study of the female anatomy could be found in the *National Geographic,* at the dentist's office. Since I had lots of cavities, I developed an inordinate interest in those photographic reports on native customs, especially the domestic customs of topless Tahitian girls bending over to grind wheat, or bending over to shape clay into pots. I never found out what native men did with their time. They just seemed to be standing around doing very much what I was doing, watching the native girls bending over.

My brother Mike's art books were another respectable source of enlightenment. Landscapes left me cold, but "The Nude Through the Ages" was just right for my age. I even made follow-up visits to the Metropolitan Museum of Art for closer study of mother-and-child paintings. (It wasn't the fat cherubs that interested me. There were at least two in my bed at home at any time.) Obviously the Renaissance masters were strong on breast-feeding. I could stand there and look to my heart's content without anybody saying "don't."

There were other sources of information about girls. The illustrations in my brother Joe's medical books were scientific but not satisfactory. I could not get enthusiastic over a cross section of a girl. Sneaking a peek across a section of the backyard into some young lady's bedroom window at nightfall was better if her light was on, the shade was up, and she didn't take too long—because it was past my bedtime and I might fall asleep at my post. (Mama often had to wake this Peeping Tom and put him to bed.) I didn't have a window shade of my own. It was not a matter of either privacy or poverty. "You don't need a window shade," Mama explained. "You're a boy. Who's gonna look at *you?*"

I even considered the possibility of being a girl for a day or two so I could check out some of my suspicions and feel what I thought a girl should feel like if I should ever get that close.

Some information reached us through the underground in the form of "naughty" jokes usually told in riddles:

"How can you tell a little girl sardine from a little boy sardine?"

"How?"

"You look and see which 'can' they come out of."

As we got older we moved on to more ribald stuff. We laughed loudly to show that we understood and were grown up. We didn't, and we weren't, but why did our friends have to know?

"You know what one little grain of wheat said to another?"

"What?"

"Help! I've been reaped!"

If I had had the temerity to tell Mama an off-color joke, my head would have come off, but the joke wouldn't. If it was a joke with a double meaning, she wouldn't have gotten either one. How far could you get with a full-grown woman who once threatened to call the police if we didn't straighten up our bedroom because she had read in the paper that a couple had been arrested for keeping a disorderly house?

I recall several futile attempts at enlarging Mama's joke repertoire.

Attempt 1: "Ma, you wanna hear a dirty joke? A boy fell in the mud."

"To you everything is funny. A boy falls in the mud, so to a loafer like you it's very funny. Because you don't have to wash his clothes it's very funny. Do you ever think of that poor woman who has to stand over a washtub in a hot kitchen and scrub the mud off the clothes of a slob like you who doesn't think of his mother . . . ?"

"Forget it, Ma."

"Forget it. For you it's easy to say 'Forget it,' because you don't have to wash his clothes. Get out of this house this minute, you dirty kid, you!"

Attempt 2: "Ma, did you hear the joke about the dirty window?"

"You don't have to clean the windows, so it's to you a big joke."

"Ma, just say, 'I didn't hear the joke about the dirty window.'"

"All right. I didn't hear the joke about the dirty window."

"Good. Because you couldn't see through it anyhow."

When Mama tried it on Mrs. Hessel, it came out this way:

"Did you hear the joke about the window you can't see through?"

"What?"

"Never mind. It's too dirty to tell anyhow."

It was not easy coming into manhood in a world in which the body made one set of demands and the antibodies of the puritan tradition made another.

I, no less than the saintly heroes of the miracle plays, was expected to smite down Temptation, Carnality, Lechery, Wantonness, Licentiousness, Sensualism, Libidinousness. Smite them? I couldn't even spell them! I was urged to vanquish the beast in me, subdue both pulse and impulse, and add the vow of chastity to the poverty I already had. I felt as if I had been chosen for Jewish priesthood. Except for the privilege of getting married some day, I had to pledge myself for the time being (however long that was going to be) to abstinence, asceticism, celibacy, and adolescent senility. By the time I would be ready for the nuptial vow I would really be fit to be tied.

"It's better if you wait," we were told.

We were used to waiting. We waited for Papa to sit down at the table before we ate, for the lighting of Sabbath candles, for new shoes, for steam heat, for a job, for money, and now for marriage—again, at the right time, in the right place, with the right girl. Everything had to be right, and right now was never right. What's your hurry? Save it for your wife. I was old enough to know what a wife was, but I still didn't know what "it" was.

What Mama was warning us against, nature was warming us up for. I was willing to wait, but I could not accept the first quickenings of my flesh as the work of the devil. It felt more like the whisperings of angels. My early vintage desire sent enough intoxicating bubbles to my brain to make me see even Flatfoot Fanny as one who walked in beauty. Had it happened to her or to me? I was getting new feelings in old places; places that only yesterday I was young enough to scratch publicly.

I had walked beside street-cleaning spray trucks before, but never till now had I noticed the purple mist they left in their wake. Out of the corner of my eye I studied my reflection in store windows and mud puddles and decided I was handsome, notwithstanding my incipient acne and my chronic dandruff. It was about then, too, that I discovered that I was not angry at Mama for all her don'ts, but sorry for her. Okay, don't is don't. But didn't she even know? And if she knew, why didn't she tell me about wild birds trapped in your undershirt, fits of silent laughter, unspeakably sweet anguish, and even a secret wish to die now before it died? Wasn't Mama ever fifteen? Didn't she ever feel this way? If not, then how did she know about all those things she had warned us against? A mother of eight kids didn't know about all this? Boy, was she underprivileged! Poor Mama!

And how about Papa? You mean, when he was fifteen he already had gas pains and sat around and cursed the boss? Didn't he ever take a walk with a girl and accidentally touch her bosom? And didn't he break out in a sweat when it happened, wondering whether if it was an accident maybe it wasn't, and maybe she had deliberately caused the accident?

And if she fell down in the grass, did he remain standing? Tell me, Papa! If you don't know, I'll tell you. Just ask me. I'll tell *you* how it feels. I have to know that you were once a boy like me, with quivering nail-bitten fingers, and that you, like me, had some doubts about the don'ts. Maybe not with Mama, but with somebody! If you'll tell me, I promise not to tell Mama.

A girl's plea to her mother that "I'm not a baby any more" brought an answer like "That's why I want you home by nine o'clock."

By the time any local girl reached her first change of life she had been so ideologically fortified against us that it was virtually impossible for any boy to break through the layers of moral dogma. She was both morally and physically impregnable. "A boy must have his fling" was not acceptable to those parents. That boy might end up flinging their daughter. Nice boys weren't supposed to disgrace decent girls, and we defined a decent girl as "one upon whom the hand of man had never set foot." A girl who "let" could also sublet. The chain of degradation started with the first let. From there it was let, let, let, down, down, down. No one would marry a girl who "let." Secondhand, slightly used merchandise was okay for our home furnishings, but the girl you marry must not be chipped, spoiled, or broken.

The general precautionary rule for girls was not to fraternize with the enemy, us, the boys. Their mothers gave them specific battle-tested techniques for self-defense:

"Just say 'No,' because before you can say 'Look here, I'd like you to know that I am not that kind of a girl,' you may already be one."

"If he says, 'Let's get married or something,' you say, 'Let's get married or nothing.' "

"If he tells you everybody is doing it, tell him *your* body isn't."

If you are really in a spot in a car on a dark street, and he is moving in on you, and all other methods have failed, don't get scared, just move real close to him, look him squarely in the eye, and say, "I think I'm gonna vomit." He won't be there very long.

❀ ❀ ❀

The sexual explosion followed close upon the atomic explosion. My sophomore's generation felt that once the bomb had been dropped by its elders, all previous don'ts became either trivial or sham-ful. The kids turned against sham and in the process also gave up shame. Shame was ours, not theirs.

The young have declared the body as the soul of the moral revolution. "Body" is not a dirty word. "Bomb," "kill," "burn," and "maim" are. Liberate the body! Liberty, Fraternity, Sexuality. Emancipate all sexual prisoners! Repeal inhibition! Democracy starts in bed! Vote early and often! Every day is a legal holiday once nothing is illegal.

Exhibition replaced inhibition. Maybe our sex was square —but not in the public square. Every meeting place has become a mating place. Just when I had gotten used to the fresh-air propagation of cats and dogs, the kids took over. The dogs and cats are now standing around watching the kids. Only heaven knows what the dumb animals will learn from the smart kids. Just wait till the animals find out that the kids don't even have a license.

❀ ❀ ❀

My generation was expected to live by a fixed morality. Our sophomore's morality is not fixed but prefixed. The prefix serves not only to modify but to mollify, even to nullify value judgments. It places the deed beyond good and evil. Today one can be *a*moral, *non*moral, *anti*moral, *neo*moral, *multi-*

moral, *super*moral, *semi*moral, *contra*moral, *quasi*moral, *ex-tra*moral. The prefix is now wagging the dogma.

The prefixes of the new sexual morality allow for a multiple choice of sexual preferences: *hetero*sexual, *bi*sexual, *homo*sexual, *super*sexual, *inter*sexual, *intra*sexual, *uni*sexual, *hyper*sexual, *contra*sexual, or *a*sexual. There are only two sexes, but the number of sex sects is infinite.

Today's free-swinging sexual morality accepts any arrangement based upon the mutual consent of one, two, or more, or less human beings. Love can be singular, plural, brotherly, sisterly, fatherly, motherly, male, female, homogenized . . .

The new "improved" family may consist of men with wives or husbands, women with husbands or wives, fathers who are not husbands, mothers who are fathers, fathers who are mothers, men who used to be women, women who used to be men. Fortunately, all seem to make a nice living appearing on public television proclaiming that their private life is none of the public's business.

Virgin girls, like virgin forests, are becoming scarce. They are being consumed faster than they can be replaced. Girls who have "never gotten married or anything" are considered to be suffering from a form of arrested development. Chastity is a condition that can ruin a girl's reputation, but is curable if detected early enough. Not to be chased is a greater disaster than not to be chaste.

Campus statistics show that while 30 percent of undergraduate women admit to being ex-virgins, 60 percent of the men admit to the same thing, which means that 30 percent of the women are looking after 60 percent of the men, which has the girls working on double shifts. The 10 percent unaccounted for are working their way through college gathering sex statistics on the 90 percent. The inactive women feel that the active ones are giving them a bad reputation, and vice versa.

There are also more pregnant brides—one of the results of

the teenage head-start program. If the bride can still zip up her wedding gown, she will not be asked to sew a scarlet letter onto her bodice. All bridal gowns are lovely so long as they arrive before Mother's Day. They do not have to be white. Pastel shades are becoming very popular. The new rules (they are more generous than the old) state that there are no premature babies, only delayed weddings.

"Repeat slowly after me: 'Do you take this woman?' "

"I did."

Between the moral climate and the room temperature in Mama's home, you couldn't stay comfortably nude for very long. People who walked around "naked" (which could mean merely no shoes, no sweater, or no scarf) were considered lunatics.

All exposure was indecent: "That's the way to talk to a boy on the telephone, in your underwear?" To see underwear meant you had seen all. "Free show!" A rip in the pants that publicly revealed pink skin or pink underwear could start a riot, especially if your "thing" was showing. "Thing" was the generic term for any part of the anatomy—back, front, upper, lower, male, female—normally hidden from view. "Thing" could also be plural, as in the expression "her 'things' were showing." The real name for "things" was considered vulgar. We stayed with such euphemisms as "thing," "toosh," "belly button."

I was there when my brother Mike brought home his first oil painting from art school—a nude. Mama didn't know whether the work was good or bad, impressionistic or realistic. She wanted to know only one thing: "Who is she?" Mike said that she was a model. Mama insisted that she was a bum. "Nice girls don't sit around like that. Tell me where she lives, I want to talk to her mother."

To strip away the "hypocrisy" of the old morality, the practitioners of the new morality went into a retaliatory striptease. To expose *us* they exposed *themselves*. We would have to face *their* naked truth. "Unzip your psyche!" "Out is 'in.' " "Don't put off until tomorrow; take it off now." "Ban the bra!" "Free the fly!" "Pan the pants!" "Bare the butt!" The fig leaves are flying. Now at last there are Three Bares: The father bare, the mother bare, and the baby bare. The family that cares, bares.

Even my old dentist has switched his magazine subscriptions from *National Geographic* to *National Pornographic*. As the years passed I have noticed an important change in literary style, especially in punctuation. The exclamation mark has become obsolete. People aren't surprised at anything any more. Also noteworthy is the fact that the same book can be listed in the library catalogue under Fiction, Clinical Psychology, Psychopathology, Bedroom Furnishings, and Popular Mechanics, but no matter what the subject, every book now has a girl on the cover and no cover on the girl. Books also come in two editions, unabridged and abridged. Unabridged means that the dirty parts have been left in; abridged means that not only have the dirty parts been left in but the clean parts have been left out. Dirty words, my sophomore tells me, are not dirty at all. They are real, earthy, true, honest. (I have to take *his* word for it.)

In the theater the classic formula for a three-act play used to be:

Act I: He wants to; she doesn't.

Act II: She wants to; he doesn't.

Act III: They both want to, so they drop the curtain and the audience politely goes home. "Exit" was the only four-letter word permitted.

In today's theater he wants to and she wants to before the play starts, but they wait until the curtain goes up, then proceed to it, with audience participation.

Proper little ladies spend twelve dollars a ticket to see something they can't believe. The shock-treatment matinée.

"Can you believe it, Gertrude?"

"I can't believe it!"

"When is the obscene scene, Mildred?"

"This is it."

"I can't believe it!"

"Stop talking. They're doing it again."

"Can you believe it?"

"Seeing is believing."

"I see it, but I still can't believe it."

The movies have also enlarged their artistic horizons to keep abreast of the 3D-cup dimensions of wide-screen nudity.

The Coming Attraction is enough to give a normal man palpitations. It's Honest! It's Beautiful! It's Carnal! It's Newd. It's Lewd. It's $4.50. *The Nymph Meets the Nymphomaniac.* Rated RX: admission by doctor's prescription only.

In the old movies intimations of intimacy were handled with the greatest subtlety. "It" was implied, insinuated, suggested, innuendoed, but never shown. We got to know the signs though. If the couple went into the woods and birds began flying madly in circles, that was "it"; a bee drawing honey out of a flower was "it"; two cigarettes left to burn out in an ashtray was "it"; also a victrola record that kept on playing in the last groove was "it."

Modern camera technique makes imagination unnecessary. The zoom lens can give a loving couple a physical that would take six days at the Mayo Clinic. The camera goes where even the X-ray fears to tread—into nostrils, eyeballs, pulsating arteries, and inner ear canals. (Amour by parts.) A bead of perspiration can be followed from her brow line down her shoulder, down her index finger, onto his vaccination. If the director runs out of ideas, he gives us a flashback of the same guy on another occasion with another bedridden girl, of whom he is reminded by this girl. He is now seen steaming through the pores next to some lung-inflated fisherman's daughter, whose oxygen supply to the brain has been cut off by his teeth in her jugular vein. They knead each other badly. Flashbacks can come at any time. He may be addressing an international scientific convention when it all comes back to him. Zoom! Instant replay!

Most of what I see appears to me not sophisticated but naïve, a bit like those early naughty stories—kid stuff, for immature audiences only. Box-office seduction of the emotionally deprived for a pornocopia of silver. Those of us who have been fortunate enough to have lived intimately with love in all of its manifestations do not need to participate in group voyeurism. Nudity on stage is not necessarily obscene. Some nudes reveal nothing but flesh; others, the soul of a human being. I am sorry for those who are being sold soul-free skin and bones as the human being. The naked truth is beautiful if it is the truth, the whole truth, and nothing but the truth, and not merely the nude, the whole nude, and nothing but. As Mama would have said: "Don't buy by him."

I have seen the current wave of sexual activism become an obsession bordering on enslavement. Our sophomore, ready or not, is driven by the need to prove himself sexually liberated. There are new tests to be passed every day, and there is no graduation day. The requirements of high frequency may instigate a loveless preoccupation with satisfying an obligation not so much to one's own body as to the bodies of more committed sextavists. It takes great courage for a Daughter of the Sexual Revolution to say, "Let me off this streetcar named Desire. I don't care to go to the last stop. Please!"

My sex education was far from ideal. It was typical of its time. Waiting was never easy (the urge was often urgent), yet I sometimes wonder whether it wasn't easier for us to suffer the pangs of waiting than to have to prove our maturity upon demand. Instant sex, like instant coffee, may not necessarily be the best. Besides, we may not need as many brands as the sex hawkers promote, any more than we need thirty-two brands of cottage cheese. It's quality we need, not quantity.

The sexual freedom fighters' "Make love, not war" is not a peace slogan but a sex slogan. If making love is to be the equivalent of love, then streetwalkers should be revered and remembered tenderly on St. Valentine's Day. If the act of lovemaking rather than the art of love is to be the summum bonum of our civilization, gynecologists should be our high priests.

I prefer a simple "Love, not war." Making love is hardly an antidote for war.

The history of man proves that he has somehow been able to find time for making love and war. Violence has not decreased with the advent of sexual freedom.

Man is as much in need of a course in remedial love as in remedial sex. Man does not live by bed alone. He has yet to bring his ethical urge up to the level of his sexual urge. Right now passion is running ahead of compassion.

When Emily started to date we talked about being beautiful. I suggested to her that the truly "beautiful people" are not necessarily in the jet set, the fashion set, the money set, or the sex set, but in the soul set. I even suggested several time-tested inexpensive beauty hints:

For attractive lips, speak words of kindness.

For lovely eyes, seek out the good in people.

For a slim figure, share your food with the hungry.

For beautiful hair, let a child run his fingers through it once a day.

For poise, walk with the knowledge that you will never walk alone.

One of these days some guy just might say, "Gee, baby, you're beautiful." He might even want to marry you.

XVII
The Prophet System
❀ ❀ ❀

I was born in one era and my sophomore in another; yet not
unlike Mama and me at Carnegie Hall, I see us both in the
same dream. Now the stage is his, but unlike me, he is not a
soloist. He performs with a group whose repertoire consists
as much of messages (poetical or political) as melodies, elec-
tronically amplified to give them greater social significance
and to make sure I get the message. They are not playing *for*
me but *at* me.

Can the old alumnus and the young sophomore ever see eye
to eye? It is not a matter of who is right (nobody is always
right, not even a freshman), but of different views of life.
My vision is double; his is single. He sees only ahead; I can
see behind and ahead. He has lived twenty years only once.
I've done it again and again, and it's been harder each time
around.

We may not always see eye to eye, but we can try to see

heart to heart. We are not at odds over the ends, but we frequently do come to a parting of the ways over the means.

We of the alumni association say he is "too" this; the undergraduate says we are "too" that. We are caught up in a variant of the "never" and "always" quarrel of married couples, except that here it is more like two monologues than a dialogue.

"You are too idealistic."

"You are too practical."

"You are too impetuous."

"You are too cautious."

"You are too defiant."

"You are too compliant."

He is young and unbending. At our age we are glad we can bend at all. We still request, propose, and recommend. We still beg to differ. He will not beg for anything. He demands.

My sophomore may be free of my hangups, but he now has his own. Mine had to do with restriction; his have to do with freedom. He has many more freedoms than I had and more free time to exercise them. He hopes to make freedom compulsory for all. (To me his new "compulsory" seems no better than my old "forbidden.") He wants to set me free, but I don't care to let *his* conscience be my guide. Freedom for me means the right to choose, at my own discretion, to be somewhat less than free, or not free at all, on behalf of some other equally precious human value, such as sacrifice or devotion, given freely for the good of some other person. "Musts" can be as joyous as "mays." Sometimes it may be better to "No thyself."

I am not convinced that "doing your own thing" necessarily represents the height of freedom, even when qualified with the disclaimer "so long as it isn't hurting anybody." I've noticed that the "anybody" one assumes he is not hurting is hardly ever consulted. Nor am I impressed by the cloak of

179

immunity called "honesty." The truth about honesty is that one can be honestly ruthless.

Gratitude is high on the list of my hangups.

My sophomore is not as accustomed to it as I am: Fank shoe, Uncle Looing . . . It's great, Ma, thanks, Ma . . . thanks for the violin lessons, for the shoes, for the education, thanks, thanks, thanks . . . I am even grateful to my courageous sophomore for urging me to stand up for what I believe. Since I believe in gratitude, I would like to borrow a little of my sophomore's courage and insist that he be grateful. If insisting on gratitude seems like an excessive demand, maybe we can call it recognition, acknowledgment, perhaps even social justice.

Since he wants me to tell it like it is, here it is in his language, in the form of a love letter from the parent body.

Darling Soph:

You were born of a parental *love-in*. Right off we got *hooked* on you, and we didn't need *LSD* to get *turned on*. You were our *thing,* and we built our *establishment* around you. We held daily *demonstrations* of our loyalty. We *resisted* all *injustices* toward you. We practiced *nonviolence* against you even under *provocation*. We held all-night *sleep-ins* at your bedside when you were sick, and there was *pot,* much pot, which we carried to and from, and when the fever went up to 104 we held a *pray-in* to *overcome*. We gave you *free love,* a wall-to-wall carpeted *pad* of your own, and the best education we could (or could not) afford. We never *freaked out* when the going was rough. Now you are ready to *remake the world* for the better. We are with you. Just one request, if we may. When the *brotherhood of man* is established, could you maybe make the membership broad enough to include motherhood and fatherhood? We want in. We want in! We, too, belong to *now,* and we cherish our *now* dearly, because we can't count on as much of it as you can. Toss us a *flower* now and then—preferably now!

Lovingly yours,
The Committee for Peace, Love, and Amnesty for Parents

My sophomore prefers to call his dreams causes. That's fine with me. Great dreams do become great causes, and great causes finally become great traditions.

We share a common cause and a common tradition. It goes way back to a moment in human history (pre-Y.C.F.C.) when some primitive cousin (whose genes we inherited) somewhere in a cave dreamed of changing from beast to man. I can see him waking the family: "Up, up, everybody. It's the dawn of a new era. Enough already with the killing. Is that the way for a man to behave?" His wife probably said, "He's been carrying on like that since he took to drinking milk."

Civilization started when this Stone Age relative began to yearn for a new morality when there was no such word as "morality," old or new. There was nobody around distributing stone pamphlets on the subject. There was not even an alphabet. There was nothing to go by but the need he felt to be loved more than to be feared. This need evoked in him what were then revolutionary intuitions, like maybe right might make might ("Don't knock it till you've tried it"); that stones might be used for building as well as for killing ("I've tried it; it works"). He may even have noticed that beasts cannot shed tears and that tears make you human. And he never even got a bronze plaque as Man of the Era at a luncheon (they had gotten to luncheons, but not yet to bronze) for his efforts on behalf of the greatest cause of all time—the debrutalization of man.

Centuries later these early premonitions became words intended not to deify man but to dignify him; magnificent words spoken in gatherings and marketplaces and temples, sometimes even shouted from mountaintops by the impassioned haranguers, agitators, teachers, preachers, apostles, disciples, and prophets of biblical Judaism and Christianity. Their words are still so relevant for our time that I would like to suggest some of them as slogans for my sophomore's banners and buttons.

Peace:
Whoso sheddeth man's blood, by man shall his blood be shed.

Genesis 9:6

Justice:
Justice and only justice shall you pursue.

Deuteronomy 16:20

One law for the native and for the stranger.

Exodus 12:49

Thou shalt not stand idly by the blood of thy neighbor.

Leviticus 19:16

Woe to them . . . that take away the right of the poor.

Isaiah 10:2

Freedom:
Proclaim liberty throughout the land unto all the inhabitants thereof.

Leviticus 25:10

Antimaterialism:
What is a man profited if he gain the whole world and lose his own soul.

Matthew 16:26

A man's life consists not in the abundance of his possessions.

Luke 12:15

Sharing:
The profit of the earth is for all . . .

Ecclesiastes 5:9

The Dignity of Labor:
Oppress not a hired servant.

Deuteronomy 24:14

Poverty:
If your brother become poor . . . you shall maintain him.

Leviticus 25:35

The fact that these great moral ideals have too often been violated and desecrated even in the name of God does not discredit them; it discredits us. They have not failed, we have.

I have not deliberately omitted the Greco-Roman, Asian, or African contributions to the cause of human nobility. It's just that Mama hardly ever quoted from those sources. For that matter, she hardly ever quoted Mark, Luke, John, or Matthew either. She only quoted Papa, a poor tailor descended from great prophets.

When I hear my sophomore denouncing materialism, racism, corruption, war, poverty, misuse of wealth and power, I remember his biblical ancestors, the early moral activists, the dissenters of their time, so often reviled, exiled, imprisoned, martyred. My ethical roots go back to them. I am a registered member of their party. That makes me a conservative radical—from the Latin *conservare*, "to keep," and *radicalis*, "having roots." I choose to keep those roots alive. My sophomore is not so much concerned with old roots as with fresh flowers. He does not always realize how much he stems from those saintly men. He believes that man's salvation is secular. "Please, God, I'd rather do it myself." His uncle, the prophet, spoke in the name of God, whose covenant with man, he insisted, is based upon man's treating his fellow-man as sacred. The prophets foresaw the degeneration of any society that lost that hallowed vision, not because God would destroy it, but because it would destroy itself. Desanctification of man, they said, leads to dehumanization of man.

So deep-rooted was this ethic that its spirit remained alive through the postbiblical era, the Middle Ages, the Renaissance, the Age of Reason, the French Revolution, the American Revolution, and my Bar Mitzvah.

On that momentous day I came into my ethical inheritance. I was presented with the rights of manhood before a packed house of menfolk, womenfolk, and kidfolk. I had to accept these rights in a speech written not by me, nor by my elders, but by tradition. I stood up and in a changing voice read my changeless rights aloud: "I now have the right to do right, to do justice, to do good, to serve humanity, to help the needy, to heal the sick, to look after my country, to strive for peace, to seek after truth, to fight oppression, to liberate all mankind from bondage . . ." As I read on I realized that I had been taken. I had fallen into a moral trap. What rights? These rights were really obligations, commitments, responsibilities. I began to catch on. My rights and obligations not only became inseparable but together formed a moral mandate, the mandate of manhood. What tradition was telling me was that responsibilities exercised by all guaranteed the rights of all, and it started with me. And to top it off, these rights were not only commandments but *privileges,* for which I had to be *grateful.*

"I want to thank you for the privilege of adult responsibility . . ."

When I finished the speech I was pelted with little bags of candy. That was the custom. The symbolism was clear. My manhood was going to be full of responsibilities, but they could be sweet.

❁ ❁ ❁

I am not bound by this tradition but freed by it to make decisions, not by such ephemeral criteria as today's fashionable "in" or "out," but on the basis of man's conscious advancement from savagery to humanity. What supports and accelerates this advancement is in the humanitarian tradition. What delays or impedes it is not.

It has helped me to resist any encroachment upon the time of my life in the interest of speed, any curtailment of human response in the interest of efficiency, any abridgment of emotional involvement in the interest of mechanization. "Look, Ma, no hands" can easily become "Look, Ma, no Sam."

In a sense I am still using Mama's remedial arithmetic. Does it increase my humanity or diminish it? Keep the increaser; cross out the diminisher. (This holds for the current abundance of political ideologies as well as for the "conveniences.") Is it kind or cruel? Choose the kind. Is it peaceful or violent? Choose the peaceful. Among the living, newborn or aged, there may be the ultimate messenger of peace the world has been waiting for; in committing violence upon even the lowliest of men you may destroy the last hope for universal peace. Perhaps (God forbid) we have already destroyed him. He may possibly be buried in some unmarked grave, or perhaps in one of the many tombs of the Unknown Soldier on either the winning or the losing side.

The "new consciousness" my sophomore's generation talks about is ancient. They have rediscovered simplicity, the sanctity of life, nature, peace, freedom. They are going back to the past, to the earth, to working with their hands, mastering ancient handicrafts, to small shops and street vending, just like the men in Mama's life. They give birth naturally, nurse their babies, and carry them on their backs. They bake bread, eat organic foods, and, like Grandma, have long lists of edibles that are kosher or not kosher according to the new ecological rules. They have even gone back to Grandma's mortar and pestle for use rather than for decoration. They are nostalgic for a past they never knew, back somewhere between the Fall and the fallout, when body and soul were one, innocent and uncontaminated.

The fashions of the future-makers are right out of the past. The "now" group looks like "once upon a time." They dress up as shepherds, troubadours, woodsmen, plowmen, pioneers, Confederate soldiers, pirates, blacksmiths, Robin Hoods, Adam and Eve, Bonnie and Clyde.

They do not believe in ritual. Like pilgrims, they come barefoot from all corners of the earth for festivals, but they do not call them pilgrimages. They will gather before an illuminated stage in the woods, but do not call it a shrine. They will partake of bread and wine, but do not call it communion. They wear peace medals, and love medals, but do not call them sacred medallions. They marry under green bowers, but do not call them canopies. They take vows, but do not call them oaths. They hold silent vigils, but do not call them retreats. They practice transcendental meditation, but do not call it prayer. They have gurus, but do not call them prophets. They will congregate for sit-ins, love-ins, and talk-ins, but do not call them congregations. They will not say "Amen," but they do say "Right on!" They have come not to the end but to the beginning of tradition. So many of our late pagans have become early Christians and even earlier Jews. Welcome home!

Many who have taken to the gospel according to Marx as a reaction against the old God-centered rites, rotes, and rituals have discovered that Marxism, too, is a religion, man-centered, but not without its own myths, signs, symbols, icons, sacred books, autos da fé, heretics, saints, deposed saints, reinstated saints, disciples, apostles, and prophets. While Marxism puts matter at the core of the universe, the Marxists are sometimes uneasy about the matter of what makes matter really matter. It comes through in their humor. When a Soviet four-year-old asked his father "Is there really no God?" his papa sighed and said, "What can I tell you my child? Only God knows."

Marxist theologians throughout the world have begun to speak of a reconciliation with Christianity. The profit system may be on the critical list, but the prophets are making a surprising recovery. The most revolutionary of revolutionary ideas to emerge in this century is that "Thy kingdom come, Thy will be done on earth as it is in Heaven" is not only compatible with socialist doctrine but the mother of it. Heaven is a just and joyous society; how about we try for it on earth?

I have watched my sophomore searching for his umbilical tie to the past at those very moments when he thought he was cutting it off. In his flight from the "middle-class tyranny" of the suburbs he has found sanctuary in the East Village—the same old East Side to which his immigrant grandfather escaped from tyranny not long ago. Our sophomore's reaching out for identification with the deprived, the oppressed, the disfranchised and dispossessed has led him back to the streets, even to the very tenements in which his immigrant grandpa fought his war of liberation. He is going to have humble beginnings even if he has to rent them. We, his parents, deprived our sophomore of the opportunity of continuing the great tradition by persuading him that in our comfortable homes all the great battles had been won, that eternal peace and tranquillity were right there in front of the TV set.

Our middle-class sophomore is overcome by the need to overcome. He has to know deprivation before he can proceed to conquer it. He needs downward mobility. Riches to rags. The chance to lower himself by his own bootstraps. Once he has "made it" he can take on Grandpa's old enemies as his own. Down with racists, bigots, exploiters! He even takes on Grandpa's traditional beard. (His father can't do that; it makes him look too young.)

A third wave of immigrants has recently turned up in the East Village—parents looking for their children who have gone looking for their parents' parents.

Many of us are looking for our children, but are they looking for us? We, Horatio Alger heroes, are no longer quite the hero-images we used to be. Sorry, wrong era. While there are some who persist in that tradition, many of the sophomore class have come to question the very compatibility of private success and public morality. They wonder whether private gain is at all possible without public loss. They see our success as guilt-edged. They dream of a world of winners without losers. Nobody should win the human race. Not the survival of the fittest, but survival for all. How Biblical can you get?

They want a cooperative rather than a competitive world. They do not yet have a blueprint, but they are moving instinctively toward coexistence, fraternity, mutuality. The mantle of Horatio Alger's hero now comes in the giant size. It is being worn by the block, the project, the community, the country, the world. Society is the hero. The whole is greater than any of its parts. I hope I'll be around long enough to see how it works out, to see whether collective Algerism can make it without individual Algerism.

The humanitarian tradition is philanthropic in its original Greek meaning: love of man. How love of man is best carried out for the good and welfare of the individual and society is superbly expressed by an old cousin (more of a poet than

Papa, but clearly in Papa's tradition), Moses Maimonides, who died in Spain in the year 1204.

These are his levels of charity:

The *first* and lowest degree is to give—but with reluctance or regret. This is the gift of the hand but not of the heart.

The *second* is to give cheerfully, but not proportionately to the distress of the suffering.

The *third* is to give cheerfully and proportionately but not until we are solicited.

The *fourth* is to give cheerfully, proportionately, and even unsolicited; but to put it in the poor man's hand, thereby exciting in him the painful emotion of shame.

The *fifth* is to give charity in such a way that the distressed may receive the bounty and know their benefactor, without their being known to him . . .

The *sixth*, which rises still higher, is to know the objects of our bounty, but remain unknown to them . . .

The *seventh* is still more meritorious, namely, to bestow charity in such a way that the benefactor may not know the relieved persons, nor they the name of their benefactor . . .

The *eighth* and most meritorious of all is to anticipate charity by preventing poverty; namely, to assist the reduced brother either by a considerable gift, or a loan of money, or by teaching him a trade, or by putting him in the way of business, so that he may earn an honest livelihood and not be forced to the dreadful alternative of holding up his hand for charity. . . . This is the highest step and the summit of charity's golden ladder.

While I was writing this book our first grandchild arrived, Georgia, daughter of Conrad and Isabella. When I first heard her cry I remembered my own firstborn's first night at home with us. He cried all night, and we didn't know what to do about it. Esther read through pages and pages of Dr. Spock trying to find out what makes babies cry. Grandma was standing in the doorway. We wouldn't allow her into the room because she might spread germs. She reluctantly kept her distance but tossed us the best advice on child-rearing we have ever had: "Put down the book and pick up the baby." That's just what I am going to do right after I finish this little note to Georgia.

Georgia baby:

We leave you a tradition with a future. The tender loving care of human beings will never become obsolete. People, even more than things, have to be restored, renewed, revived, reclaimed, and redeemed, and redeemed, and redeemed . . . Never throw out anybody.

Remember, if you ever need a helping hand, you'll find one at the end of your arm. As you grow older you will discover that you have two hands. One for helping yourself, the other for helping others. While I was growing up I took as many hands as I gave. I still do.

Your good old days are still ahead of you. May you have many of them.

At our age we doubt whether we will make it to your wedding, but if you remember us on that day, we shall surely be there. Mazel tov . . . mazel tov . . . mazel tov . . .